DONMAR

T.S. ELIOT FESTIVAL

20 November 2008 - 17 January 2009

The **Family Reunion**

Four Quartets

Murder *in the* Cathedral

The Cocktail Party

Readings of Eliot's Verse

including The Waste Land

D1325091

T.S. Eliot Festival is presented in association with Faber & Faber

Principal Sponsor

BARCLAYS CAPITAL

GRANTA

12 Addison Avenue, London W11 4QR
email editorial@granta.com
To subscribe go to www.granta.com or call 020 8955 7011

ISSUE 103

ISBN 978-1-905881-03-1

Black Orchids

GILLIAN SLOVO

Author of ICE ROAD,
shortlisted for the ORANGE PRIZE

Set in Ceylon and Britain of the 1950s across two
generations of a family – a powerful and moving novel
about the search to feel at home in your skin.

Available from Virago in November

virago.co.uk

CONTENTS

the Dublin Review

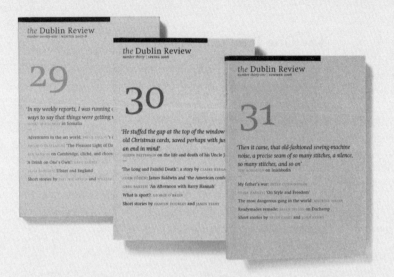

The Dublin Review is a quarterly magazine of essays, criticism, travel writing, reportage and fiction, by first-rate writers from Ireland and elsewhere: John Banville, Angela Bourke, Ciaran Carson, Amit Chaudhuri, Brian Dillon, Anne Enright, Michel Faber, Roy Foster, Tessa Hadley, Seamus Heaney, Michael Hofmann, Kathleen Jamie, Claire Keegan, Derek Mahon, Paul Muldoon, Cees Nooteboom, Andrew O'Hagan, Ruth Padel, Glenn Patterson, Tim Robinson, Ian Sansom, George Szirtes, Colm Tóibín and many more.

'an Irish institution' *Guardian*

To learn more about us, read pieces from the magazine, and subscribe, please visit our website:

www.thedublinreview.com

The Dublin Review, P.O. Box 7948, Dublin 1, Ireland

The rise of the British Jihad

Since the London bombings of July 7, 2005, in which fifty-two people were murdered in suicide attacks by Islamic terrorists, Britain has become a more troubled, less confident and harmonious country. We have witnessed an increase in Islamophobia. A generation of politically engaged writers and novelists has abandoned the liberalism of their earlier years to become, among other things, robust supporters of President Bush's war on terror. The Labour government has introduced a series of draconian counterterrorism measures, including most recently extending the right of the police to hold terror suspects without charge for forty-two days. Meanwhile, some moderate Muslim leaders refuse to accept that the various bomb plots in which young British Muslim men have been arrested for scheming to blow up airlines, shopping centres and nightclubs are in fact real.

Does all this mean the terrorists are winning? Certainly spectacular acts of terrorism have succeeded in altering the consciousness of our age; in changing the way we think, act and dream. 'Terror,' wrote Don DeLillo in his novel *Mao II*, 'makes the new future possible'.

What of that future? If the recent past is anything to go by, it will be profoundly unstable; nor is there any doubt that before too long there will be another murderous attack on Britain from within Britain. For the record, there are at least 200 indigenous active terrorist cells being monitored by the Security Service MI5, with 4,000 British Muslims considered to be a threat to national security.

The story of the rise of the British jihad is one of labyrinthine complexity and as yet it naturally has no ending. (More information may emerge about the relationships of the various Islamist plotters over the months ahead as

several important trials come to an end.) But it has a beginning – at least in the story told by Richard Watson in this issue of *Granta* – and it is in the early-to-mid-1990s when a small group of radical clerics first arrived to live and work in Britain. Among them were Omar Bakri Mohammed and Abu Qatada, who had both been expelled from countries in the Middle East, and yet once settled in London they were, without restriction from the state, free to set up networks, to preach violent jihad and to radicalize a generation of disaffected Muslim men. Many of these young men were, and still are, suspended unhappily between the country of their birth to which they feel no loyalty or natural affinity, and their ancestral homelands, which their fathers and grandfathers had left in the decades after the Second World War in search of security and a new life at the heart of the old imperial power.

Today Omar Bakri Mohammed is living in Lebanon and is banned from returning to Britain; Abu Qatada continues to live in London, but although he has never been convicted of terrorist offences he wears an electronic tag and a court order forces him to remain at home for twenty-two hours of each day. But even though neither man is free to operate as he once did in Britain, he might feel that his best work has been done. After all, there is an entire generation of British Muslims, influenced or radicalized by the clerics and their followers, who are at large in the country and determined to carry on the struggle for violent jihad in the name of the one true God, Allah.

This is my last issue as editor of *Granta*; at the end of September I will become editor of the *New Statesman*. I joined *Granta* on September 1, 2007 and since then we have relaunched and redesigned the magazine and developed a new website and online magazine, Granta.com. It has been a thrilling, often exhausting, but always happily absorbing period. My successor will be my present deputy, Alex Clark, the first woman to edit the magazine. I wish her well in the role and would like to thank all those who read, contributed to or worked on the magazine during my time as editor. ∎

Free to write, free to be

I had a farm in Africa. Or rather, my mother's family, the Bothas, had it from the 1940s until the 1990s, and it was the wrong type of farm: not Blixen's bucolic liberal ideal, but an unprofitable, insular dustpan in the Afrikaner heartland of South Africa's old Transvaal, near Rysmierbult (Termite Hill). If the adjacent districts of Krugersdorp and Roodepoort were the Afrikaner Bible Belt, then Rysmierbult could be called the buckle – the men on the farm were always loosening theirs to piss outside. This was Boer territory, where the men were *manne* and the women were supposed to produce children for the *manne*, and *koeksusters* for the church bazaar. In fact, though, my grandfather, Oupa Frikkie Botha, was not really a farmer at all, but a schoolteacher of Latin and maths with a dangerous fondness for Virgil. Hence the farm. And, as it turned out, he couldn't do the maths. In spite of generous government subsidies, the *mielies* didn't multiply. The sheep didn't fatten. The peaches rotted. The dream of rural self-sufficiency failed.

The farm, impecunious and touchingly ridiculous, has long since been sold; but before it went it became, for me, the embodiment of a way of life, a phase in the development of Afrikanerdom, that has also passed. A phase, necessarily, in my own development, because I started life as an Afrikaner, and as an Afrikaans speaker. My father was a career diplomat whose stint in the foreign service began in Pretoria in the Verwoerd years. It would take us back there in the 1980s, just as apartheid was

entering its last and most violent phase, via the USA (where I was born in 1969), Israel, Germany and England. During this period my uncle – Oupa Frikkie's third son, Pik – was the South African foreign minister. In the 1940s my father's father, a van Niekerk, had been the National Party's first MP for what was then South West Africa (now Namibia). And my father himself ended his career as Deputy Director General of Foreign Affairs under de Klerk. We were, by any definition, part of the Afrikaner establishment – what the writers Hans Strydom and Ivor Wilkins have dubbed the 'Super Afrikaners'.

When I was growing up in the 1970s and early 1980s we would visit the Botha farm every year from whichever country we were in at the time. It seemed a place apart from the world, sealed in a golden noonday doze among the *mielie* fields and the peach orchards. While my grandfather failed at farming my grandmother presided over the farmhouse, a cool honeycomb of stone and corrugated iron kept going by smiling servants who lived in a separate compound of mud huts. My uncles and teenage cousins would arrive in *bakkies* and clouds of yellow dust and would spend the days drinking, hunting and arguing about politics. They all seemed unfeasibly tall and had bass voices and bare feet. There was a round dam, covered in weeds and pooling slime, where we swam. We ate copiously: the kitchen was lined with vast blue enamel bins of sugar, salt, flour, rice and oats; the fridge was full of bacon, lamb and *wors*; joints of drying kudu meat dangled from the rafters of the pantry. We trod the *traporrel* (an organ) in the dining room and sang folk songs: '*My Hartbeeshuis*', '*Vat Jou Goed en Trek*', '*Daar Kom Tant Alie*'. At night we slept behind a grilled iron door. Around us the country was going up in flames (literally: in 1980 the Sasol oil refinery was blown up by Umkhonto we Sizwe not many miles away). And everyone spoke Afrikaans.

Afrikaans, with its gravelled Gs, trilling Rs and explosive plosives, was the first indigenous language in South Africa to evolve from a purely spoken to a published and literary language. Having developed from the seventeenth-century Dutch imported by the earliest white settlers, with an infusion of Portuguese, French, Malay and African languages such as Xhosa and Zulu, it is still the first language of about three million whites and perhaps a further two million coloured and black South Africans. For decades it was intimately bound up with the legalized racial discrimination of apartheid. Founded on the Calvinism of a pastoral people, with a hell of a sociological kick provided by the idea of predestination, apartheid was as dependent for its codes on Afrikaans as it was on the Afrikaners themselves. Attack Afrikaans and you automatically attack the Afrikaner – the schoolchildren rioting in Soweto in 1976, in protest at the government's decision to impose Afrikaans as the language of instruction for half the subjects taught in non-white schools, grasped that instinctively. Reverence for the language was also an unspoken rule both on the farm and in our house. Being Afrikaans speakers was what we, as Afrikaners, were.

My paternal grandfather and my uncle (*Oom*) Pik belonged to that immense clandestine Freemasons' network, the Afrikaner Broederbond; my formidable aunt (*Tannie*) Elize was a scholar in Afrikaans literature and linguistics, president of several Afrikaans language foundations, Chancellor of the Afrikaans-medium Stellenbosch University and a director of the Nasionale Pers (National Press). None of us seriously questioned the ideals of apartheid or its fantasy of absolute racial and linguistic self-determination. Afrikaans played a key role in this fantasy: it was the vehicle for the formulation of a Christian national civil religion and an equally pernicious and limited segregated educational system.

When the time came for me to begin my formal education, however, we were living in Tel Aviv in Israel. The only viable school for miles around was the American School. With amazing fortitude, my parents bit the bullet and taught me a form of Afrikaans-inflected pidgin English in three weeks flat. I have spent the last thirty-odd years trying to learn English. I had some initial help from the British Embassy School in Bonn, where we went next, which sanded down my Americanisms, and later from St Paul's Girls' School in London, which buffed up what was left. I was an English speaker when, at the age of thirteen, I returned to Pretoria's airless, jacaranda-lined suburbs. My cousins called me a *rooinek* (redneck). In return I refused to speak Afrikaans. I went straight into the Pretoria High School for Girls, a grand neoclassical dungeon established by Lord Milner in 1902 to anglicize the Afrikaner. In my case he could have spared himself the trouble: I was already anglicized. And yet, whatever I was, I wasn't English. Though English-speaking South Africans invariably took me for what they reverently called a 'real Brit', the English in England weren't fooled for an instant. Those flat vowels, the suspicious ability to pronounce vulgar gutturals – no, it just wouldn't wash.

But back in South Africa I no longer belonged to the Afrikaner clan, the tribe, and what set me apart, far more so than my foreign childhood or any acquired differences in ideology, was the simple fact that I now spoke English as my mother tongue. It is impossible to adopt an entirely new language as a child without also becoming a new person. There is a sense in which the language we speak, with its compacted accommodations with history, its nuances of meaning and underlying cultural assumptions, speaks us. English – and not the attenuated, semantically impoverished form of English, stuffed with malapropisms and misuses, preferred by English

'*Sarf Effrikkens*', but the English of the metropolis – offered me a chance to be a radically different self.

Unlike many other South Africans, I didn't leave apartheid South Africa for political reasons or similarly noble reasons of conscience. I returned to England in 1992 because I missed it, simply, and because I belonged here. England was the home of English, and since English had become my language, for better or worse, it was my home also. I knew, too, that I was going to write and that I couldn't do this in South Africa. There's a sense in which writing is simply scar tissue, the attempt to create a meaningful self out of a compromised one, and in my case this damage was caused by the constant move from country to country, which made for radical instability. J.M. Coetzee once characterized South African literature in the era of apartheid as 'a less than fully human literature, unnaturally preoccupied with power and the torsions of power'. This was not the sort of book I wanted to write. It's perhaps no coincidence that, once in England, I ended up working for the *Oxford English Dictionary*, and that the idea for my first novel came to me while I was filing word slips in the quotations room – in the maw of the English language, I liked to think. Repositioning myself as an English speaker in England had set me free: free to write, free to be.

Afrikaans shucked off its immediate pariah status with the advent of full democracy in South Africa in 1994, but it retains its ambiguous political and social status as a conservative, mostly white language. There are signs that it is gradually expanding to embrace what would once, in the apartheid era, have been considered 'impure' locutions, including foreign and English loanwords. What on earth will the result be? Engfrikaans?

The members of my family have reached their own various forms of accommodation with the new South Africa. It fell to

my father to organize Nelson Mandela's inauguration in 1994. In footage of the event he's the serious, greying man greeting Hillary Clinton et al. as they arrive at the Union Buildings. He retained the links he made during his years in government and is now a strategic management consultant who still writes indignant letters to, for instance, Audi, when they send him advertising in English only instead of in both English and Afrikaans. Oom Pik was Minister for Mineral and Energy Affairs under Mandela until 1996, when he retired. He joined the ANC in 2000 and spends most of his time on his farm writing poetry. Tannie Elize became chairman of the commission responsible for designing the New South African flag (those 'ethnic Y-fronts'), and continued to advise the Mandela and Mbeki governments on cultural affairs. She died last November after serving as Chancellor of Stellenbosch University for nine years.

My cousins, too, have moved on: Oom Pik's son Piet Botha is better known in South Africa as the bilingual rock singer Jack Hammer, while Pik's daughter Lien is an artist producing sensitive visual interrogations of what it means to be an Afrikaner and an African – the intersection, you could say, between a private and a national history – which have won her considerable critical respect in the country. Another cousin was blown up in 1983 during the Angolan Civil War. A fourth flies planes for the South African Defence Force. A fifth is a gay florist. Another is a forensic pathologist; another, a fellow of the Council for Scientific and Industrial Research. And so on. They are all committed to South Africa. For me, though, it is too late. England and the English language have claimed me, lock, stock and barrel. Like many other children of apartheid, I have come to accept that, just as it is possible to speak Afrikaans and yet not be an Afrikaner, it is also entirely possible to be an Afrikaner and not speak, or write in, Afrikaans. ■

The flawed cartographer

S ometime after the first Gulf War, I heard on the news that
sixty-three per cent of young Americans could not identify
Iraq on a map of the world. I could tell by the way that the presenter
spoke that this was something bad: more evidence that Americans
were silly. I spent a moment thinking where Iraq was. My mind
was blank. This worried me. I didn't want to be sneered at by
newsreaders so I tested myself by drawing a map of the world.

Britain and Ireland started off pretty well. Australia, way over
on the far edge of the paper, was also good. But beyond that, things
started to get a little amorphous. I knew what individual countries
such as Spain and Italy looked like, but the shape of the European
land mass from which they dangled was less clear.

Just as thinking too much about words can cause them to
disintegrate into abstract plosives and fricatives untethered to
any meaning, I suspected that my mental image of the globe was
falling apart under the scrutiny of my attention. I was sure that as
a reasonably educated adult with an A in my Geography O level,
a representation of the world was burned on my brain somewhere,
even if only at a subconscious level. As I continued to draw, I let
instinct take over.

The result was quite alarming. When I showed my map to
my partner he thought it was a joke and referred to it as a Mappa
Mundi, though I now realize that did a great disservice to those
plucky medieval efforts. Most countries remained unidentified
and unnamed and the continental land masses were hideously

contorted. Africa in particular was withered down to a sorry sock, looping under Italy to meet up with Spain. The ghost of Adolf Hitler would have been delighted to see that Germany spread over most of central Europe, expanding to fill any areas of uncertainty like a Teutonic airbag. I couldn't pinpoint close European neighbours, much less anything further afield. The single worst error was Poland. It costs me a great deal to admit that I had somehow been led to believe by its name that Poland was very near the North Pole.

That was over a decade ago. In the intervening years I've worked hard to improve my knowledge of geography. I've travelled a fair bit. I have an enormous world map on the wall in my house which I stare at in the hope it will form an impression on my mind. Every now and again I have another go at drawing the world. It's better now, but still, I fear, capable of provoking a newsreader's smirk. Obviously I don't like to think that my ignorance is born of insularity and cultural arrogance – it seems to apply as much to countries I've visited as to countries I haven't; as much to the cultures I take in as those I'm indifferent to.

One of the consequences of my attempts at cartography has been to make me view all maps with some suspicion. Having seen how subjective and idiosyncratic our world view can be (okay, my world view in particular), I'm wiser to the choices made by map makers. Wounded by the derision that my original map invited, I tend now to question the authority of others and, peevishly, to criticize their efforts.

I like to focus my scorn not on the obviously controversial choice of projection, but rather on more subtle questions of representation. I notice, for example, how cartographers deliberately use soothing tones to attempt to disguise the intensely contentious and political nature of their work. The colour palette

used by world maps evokes that same simple universe glimpsed
in old Ladybird books. What disorder can there be in a world
with countries of Germolene pink, Caramac tan and Parma Violet
mauve? Perhaps we might become distracted by the faded drabs
and daydream about a new world order based on alliances between
countries of the same colour. On my map that would create a union
between the UK, Russia, Saudi Arabia and Spain pitched against
the USA, France, the Democratic Republic of Congo and Australia.
Perhaps we might believe that colours never bleed across borders.

Ordnance Survey maps are no better. They too have their own
dark agenda: to propagate an idealized vision of Britain as Trumpton.
A land of town halls, churches and post offices, the choice of
landmarks as reassuring as it is arbitrary. A more accurate reflection
might replace post offices with fried misery-chicken outlets, town
halls with all-you-can-eat buffets and the delicate Pointillist rendering
of scree with the Abstract Impressionist daubs of fly-tip sites. Perhaps
my map placed Cuba on the wrong side of America, but at least I
didn't pretend Chippy Minton was still on call.

I sneer also at the two-dimensionality of maps. The missing
third dimension of depth is less debilitating than the missing
fourth of time. I grew up and continue to live in Birmingham,
a city where a marked lack of sentimentality for the past and a
relentless programme of redevelopment mean that landmarks
can disappear overnight, road systems mutate daily. This is not a
city that can be described by an *A–Z*. Here the successful urban
navigator needs an innate sense of direction that can function
without the crutches of buildings or streets. Like a Navajo tracker
you learn to pick up on other less ephemeral, more lasting signs:
the silhouette of a certain tree, the paths of rivers and canals, the
confluence of drunks on a favoured bench.

But though I work hard at it I can't really believe in my own

VISUAL THINKING | CATHERINE O'FLYNN

contempt. Despite their flaws and my own bitter desire to find fault, I have to concede that there is ultimately something brave and admirable about maps, something that will always elevate them above the narrow alternatives. Online route-finders and satnav systems offer strangely tunnelled perspectives on the world, giving information only on a need-to-know basis, concealing more than they show. Maps lay out their naked visions of the world for all to see, providing not one route but many and revealing above all a glimpse of the flawed cartographers behind them. ■

In Gikuyu, for Gikuyu, of Gikuyu

Nairobi, Kenya

In the year 2000 I landed home, for my mother's funeral, and found myself in the small steamy office of some security official at Mombasa airport. I did not have a yellow fever certificate. A group of red-eyed bureaucrats had cornered me as I picked up my luggage. I tried to plead, using my mother's death, patriotism, Kiswahili, hand-wringing. *Ah bana, please,* I said, head tilting sideways, *Boss, Chief, Mkubwa, Mzee, Mamsap, Sir*: but there was no yield. A long shabby man just stared at me, smiling. So I reached into my pocket and gave him one hundred dollars. Then I walked away, leaving them smirking behind me.

In 2003, less than a month after the general election, in which the Kenya African National Union was swept from power for the first time since independence, I walked through the airport in Nairobi and found to my surprise that all the officials smiled, said hi, welcomed me home. *Where are you coming from?* a smiling woman asked me. *Many people are coming home now.* If I asked anybody, of any tribe, *So, how are things?* I could expect a relatively consistent answer, sometimes gossip – *They stole the mayor's chain.* We were the most optimistic country in the world. Much bar talk was even sympathetic towards former President Moi – people were angry that, during the inauguration of the new government, the crowds, the largest in Kenya's history, had thrown mud at Moi. How unseemly. There were stickers with the flag everywhere.

If you carry a Kenyan passport, and are leaving Kenya to go to London, with a valid visa, on our national carrier, there is a particular little humiliation you need to go through: you are pulled aside by somebody from the carrier and asked to explain why you need to go to London. You are asked questions and your passport is photocopied and examined closely.

Tourists with better geopolitics sail past you.

So, one day, about two years ago, well into Mwai Kibaki's first season as president, a young woman with a good middle-class accent looked at my passport, then looked at me, then looked at my passport, then looked at me, and asked, *What tribe are you?* I was startled. Something was wrong with this question. She manifested no tribe at all in her body language or in her spoken English. She was just some young Nairobi girl in an air hostess's uniform. In many years of flying, nobody had ever asked me what tribe I belonged to. This is not to say that tribe did not matter. It is easy enough to tell who shares your mother tongue, and what you do is chat casually in your mutual language, in low voices – all of us conscious, for no clear reason, that this is a way of dealing between ourselves, and is okay, but can be shameful if it is too public.

So I thought that maybe this young woman was not serious. I asked her, jokingly, whether the authorities in England had blacklisted Gikuyus.

No, she laughed. *But... this name of yours, Binya-Minya-Faga, where is it from?*

She was smiling her air-hostess smile, head tilted to the side.

Nakuru, I said, naming my hometown.

In fact, the name Binyavanga originates from Uganda. Nakuru is a Kenyan town, but I was not about to make this easy for her.

She jabbed me happily. *Ha ha,* she said, *ha ha, you are sooo funny, but, really, where is that name from? I just want to know.*

I switched to Kiswahili. This was easy enough to deal with in stern Kiswahili.

My sister, I said, looking very brotherly and concerned about her manners, *yaani, what is your business with this?*

Kiswahili is perfect for revealing unreason. If you fail with this approach, then real shit is coming.

Are you doubting that I am a Kenyan? I looked at her straight in the eye. In Kiswahili, this is devastating.

She was taken aback, and started to backtrack. The queue behind me was becoming impatient.

Oh. No. Ai! You mean it is wrong to ask? Kwani, I can't just ask you? I am just asking.

She still did not let me move. Finally I asked if she was saying I couldn't check in until I answered the question. She pouted, and let me pass. For a second I saw her ethnicity in her small sneer.

My first name, Binyavanga, has always been a sort of barometer of public mood. As a child, I hid it, and was comfortably Kenneth Wainaina. In the third form, I decided to abandon the name Kenneth. Some small humiliation had taken place. Some American guests of my father's had visited, and I had been introduced, hand forward, *This is Kenneth.*

In my own mind, Kenneth was a good Kenyan name. Not too common, like John, or Peter. Not aspirational, like the three sons of an army major in my school: Dionysus, Anestus and Marius. Or comical, like the guy who told me his name was Polycarp, and I should just call him Poly. Kenneth was a quiet, serious person who liked The Famous Five and The Three Investigators and who resented his parents' recent rejection of pork sausage and boiled egg breakfasts for things such as fermented millet porridge; he hated the smell of boiling *njahi* beans. The world, the good world,

was made of milkshake, baked beans and oats porridge. But the shilling had fallen, and my mother no longer shopped at Supaduka, which had things like leg of lamb. Now she went to the market, talked about fresh produce and stopped on the sides of roads to buy us roast maize instead of chips and sausages.

Many Kenyans, who had no class at all, called me Kennedy. Civil servants especially. I would say Kenneth. They would say, *Oh, Kennedy.*

So, we sat there, in the Rift Valley Sports Club, all dressed in the best Deacons had to offer. (Deacons was to middle-class mothers of Kenya almost like Marks & Spencer – it promised satisfactory cotton underwear for the Commonwealth's middle classes.) Then the American woman said, *Oh, Kenneth is such a lovely name, did you know it means 'handsome' in Scottish?* I blushed. I must have been about fourteen, and blushing meant all my pimples lighting up like flashlights on my forehead.

Now, I had defeated my geography teacher in an argument about the longest river in the world. I knew the word *lacustrine.* I could read a Harold Robbins novel in three hours. I had been asked to read my first-form composition to fourth formers. They had accused me of plagiarizing James Hadley Chase. I was mortified: I was too intelligent to read James Hadley Chase.

I was a smug and self-satisfied little shit.

And this woman knew my name better than I did.

So, I became Binyavanga Wainaina. I had moved to Mangu High School, where smart kids from all over the country came to study. In truth, I got into the school because the headmaster was tongue-tied while talking to my beautiful and exotic mother. He could not say no. I was Kenyan enough, with a dash of exoticism. There was some 'international' in me. Uganda was well mythologized. We had a physics teacher, a victim of the war in

Uganda, who had a PhD.

In the ragged and nerdy school, with people meeting people from other tribes for the first time, nobody struggled to *pronounce* my name. I was a bit strange, but we were all a bit strange.

While I was in A levels, somebody gave me a copy of *Decolonizing the Mind* by Ngugi wa Thiong'o and fancied myself an intellectual. The book impressed me because it used words like *decolonizing*. A very satisfying word: like a squeegee on a dirty dorm floor, it promised to leave things squeaky clean. We are not messy people, it said, you can pull a completely unpolluted person out of the mush. I was terribly impressed. So I decided to name myself with Gikuyu correctness.

My father's proper Gikuyu name is Muigai, but people know him as Job Wainaina. Wainaina is not my father's name. It is my grandfather's. But the confusion of the British naming system inserted itself into the way we register our names, and left many strange parallel ways of announcing yourself. You had to have a *surname*. So, my grandfather's name became our family surname. In a culturally decentralized society such as that of the Gikuyu, names are used to plot you, quite exactly, on a map. You can ask a stranger three questions, and know where he or she comes from, which clan they belong to.

I was not brave enough to decolonize myself. Removing the Wainaina would be to separate myself from my nuclear family, from my father, and to place myself in our family roots in Kanyariri village, a place I do not know at all. We are the Wainainas of Nakuru, and that mattered to me.

Anyway, it would be stupid to go around telling people my name is Binyavanga wa Wainaina because then they would grin and start nattering away in Gikuyu and my fakeness would be exposed. If they did not belong to my tribe, or to the more

anglicized middle classes, they would look at me as if I were one of those communist Mau Mau-loving people who do not date women in perms, curly kits and lipstick. I wanted to date women in curly kits and lipstick. You do not slouch about Wimpy restaurants looking like Shabba-Doo or Boogaloo Shrimp or Michael Jackson and call yourself Binyavanga wa Wainaina. You do not go to Bubbles nightclub and say to some chick, *Hi, my name is Binyavanga wa Wainaina.*

The problem with decolonizing is that it reveals you to be undecolonizable.

So Binyavanga Wainaina stuck. Not a single person throughout the Moi era asked me directly why I was called Binyavanga. People were curious, but they investigated subtly. Sometimes I would say my full name, and people would smile politely and say a small, *Oh?*

And somebody standing next to me, who knew me, would say, *His mother is Ugandan.* Or, *Ah, you know these days people are from all over.*

Now, after the incident with the air hostess, three years into Kibaki's reign in Kenya, my name mysteriously started to twist tongues. *Binyawho? Manyabanga?* Sometimes people started laughing at it. All the people who were unable to pronounce my name were Gikuyus. My own tribe. Some members of my family. Friends even. One person stopped me on a street to tell me how happy they were when they saw me in the newspaper, but that name of yours, my friends are asking, *You are half what?*

For the first time in my life, to be Gikuyu was a public event. You were tagged and measured, and then people let you in. There was a national conversation taking place and this conversation was happening in Gikuyu, for Gikuyu and of Gikuyu.

The rest of Kenya became *The Tribes.* Or *Beasts from the West.* This sort of thing was being peddled even among the middle

classes. The direct target of this was the Luo, personified by Raila
Odinga, then leader of the Orange Democratic Movement and
now Prime Minister in the coalition government, who became
the devil in hundreds of text messages and websites. For decades,
the public face of Kenya's struggle for identity has been symbolized
by towering Gikuyu politicians fighting towering Luo politicians.
In our vague, unthinking way, we Gikuyus have come to see the Luo
as meaning the coming of communism, emotionalism and the
collapse of order.

To be Gikuyu, it is now being said every day in nearly every
forum where Gikuyus gather, is to be reasonable. We are the invisible
middle-class objectivity of Kenya. For others to belong among us,
they have to behave like us. We do not need to examine ourselves.

We need to tame the tribes.

Years ago an old man I respect told me that Kenya would work
wonderfully if we had an overt policy to develop people according
to their tribal abilities. Positive tribalism, he called it. The Luhya
are strong, and make good labourers; they also speak English very
well. The Luo are very artistic and creative. They are good tailors.
The Kamba make good soldiers, because they are loyal. So the
man went around the pizza that is Kenya, naming every slice
and according it grace. It completely escaped him that every skill
coincided near-perfectly with the first acts of labour division
introduced by the British; that he was, in fact, affirming exactly
how we were defined and given roles to play in colonial Kenya.
These identities were, to him, our permanent tribal personality.
I asked him, *So what will the Gikuyu do in this utopian Kenya?*
He was surprised, and frowned. It had not occurred to him.
The Gikuyu just *were*, and everybody else was an ethnic.

Something slipped into his generation's view of a possible
Kenya. Those early Gikuyu technocrats under Kenyatta inherited

almost exactly the British idea about who does what: who runs things, who can, who can't and why not. The tribes were primeval and could not escape their fate. This impartial and objective view is always presented as the conclusion of a long and thorough analysis that, by complete coincidence, comes up with the finding that we are the best people to allow the tribes to develop.

Over the past four years, many Kenyans complained that nice middle-class Gikuyus were meeting in office corridors and speaking in their language. It was a strangely disturbed place to be: many Kenyans assumed I was not Gikuyu and would share their concerns with me. An equal and opposite paranoia about the Gikuyu was starting to spread around Kenya. By the December general election of 2007, Gikuyu had become cockroaches and weeds. Many Gikuyus spoke of their newly discovered contempt for everybody else. The mood was triumphant. We are back! And now Kenyatta is on the face of the Kenya shilling again!

It is clear that this sort of ethnic chauvinism has been growing all over Kenya, with all tribes, and the terrible post-election violence of earlier this year was the inevitable culmination of this new reality. The most visible Gikuyus in Kenya said nothing about the rising sense of a Gikuyu establishment. Our new cardinal took, exclusively, his tribe's position in the political debates last year.

Of the older generation, hardly anybody credible was speaking to the idea that we were better than the political rhetoric. Nobody was prepared to admit that their own tribe had anything to account for. To publicly criticize ourselves was to give the enemy a weapon to use against 'us'. We had all gone mad. It was left for us to assume that the elders had closed ranks to make sure a Luo was not elected president in the December general election. For it has come to be, now, that part of what it means to be a Gikuyu is not to be a Luo. ∎

A shining monument of loss

M y grandmother was not my grandmother. I started referring to her as my grandmother only in the United States because I was too lazy to explain how she had come to mean what she meant to me. Other than a couple of years before her death, she spent her whole life in Bosnia, mostly in Sarajevo. Her name was Jozefina, but I could not pronounce it when I was a kid, so I called her Teta-Sina (Auntie Sina). Her husband's name was Martin, but I called him Raro, because I could not pronounce his name either.

Raro died under siege. He just keeled over from a stroke, while sitting on a sofa. Every time I went to Sarajevo after the war – almost always staying with Teta-Sina – she would describe to me in detail how he died. She would often sit in the same place on the sofa where he had sat when he died and she would show me how he put his head down, said, 'I am not well', and died.

And then she would tell me what a good husband he had been and how he would make coffee and serve it to her every morning. She liked to tell me about the only four fights they had ever had in their life together. The first time was when they were dating (which, back before the Second World War in the small Bosnian town where they had met, meant exchanging coy glances and flirting): she got mad at him because he offered candy to some other girl. She got muddled and sidetracked while telling me about their second fight, so I don't remember what it was about. The third time they fought was when Martin got upset because she did not wash his socks when he asked her to, so they were not

dry before he had to go to work. The fourth fight was relatively serious: he blamed her for spoiling their son Božidar, who failed his university exams and lost a year. Four fights in fifty years – that was my weekly average at the time.

Božidar (whose name translates as 'God's gift') was once saved from drowning by an angel. Time and time again Teta-Sina would tell me how a pale young man in white underwear pulled little Božidar out of the river and carried him in his arms to her. After Martin died, Božidar had a cardiac arrest and was clinically dead for some minutes, surviving only because she had insisted he went to the hospital, as her instinct was telling her something was wrong.

Božidar died a few years later, and Teta-Sina could not stop mourning him. Her remaining daughter, Marija, lived in Split, Croatia, so Teta-Sina spent most of her days alone in Sarajevo, replaying her life, unimaginable and unrememberable without Martin and Božidar. As a devout Catholic she prayed every day for God to take her, so she could join them in heaven.

In 1962, after my parents had finished college and married, they moved to Sarajevo and rented a small room at Jozefina and Martin's. They became very close to them, so when I was born, I was well loved by everyone – my mother still believes that it was then that I got irreparably spoiled. During my post-war visits to Sarajevo, Teta-Sina would reminisce, sipping the morning coffee, about the time when my parents were moving out and I, still a toddler, would hold on to the furniture and scream, as I did not want to leave. My parents had to bring me over every day after they had moved out or I would have gone crazy. Teta-Sina liked to tell me how we would all gather for Christmas, her and Martin's family and all the people who they considered family, and she would recall everyone's perks, the food they liked, the jokes they told. I remembered those Christmas days too when, after the feast,

over coffee and cake, the ritual demanded that stories be told in which I featured, when I ran naked around the flat before my night-time bath, or when I held on to the furniture.

The last time I visited Teta-Sina in Sarajevo before she went to live (and die) in Split, she gave me a coffee set, engraved in a traditional Bosnian fashion, that Raro had received from his company at his retirement. She thought I should have it, so I have it. Though I drink Bosnian coffee every morning – including now, as I write – I've never once used this set. If I were to use it, I would have to empty it of all that is inside it, as in a Zen parable, and what is inside it cannot – must not – be got rid of.

There are no physical objects that I wish to possess. An object either has a history or it doesn't. If it doesn't I don't care about it. If it does, it is the history of people whose lives and deaths irradiated it. Therefore I am either indifferent to the objects that surround me or they are shining monuments of some irreversible loss. This world is but a world of mourning, and there are no other worlds. ∎

The Woman in the Moon

Darlings, I write to you from the moon
where I hide behind famous light.
How could you think it was ever a man up here?
A cow jumped over. The dish ran away with the spoon.

What reached me here were your prayers, griefs,
here's the craic, losses and longings, your lives
so brief, mine long, long, a talented loneliness.
I must have a thousand names for the earth, my blue vocation.

Round I go, the moon a diet of light, sliver of pear,
wedge of lemon, slice of melon, half an orange, onion;
your human music falling like petals through space,
the childbirth song, the lover's song, the song of death.

Devoted as words to things, I stare and stare;
deserts where forests were, vanishing seas. When your night comes,
I see you staring back as though you can hear my *Darlings,
what have you done, what have you done to the earth?*

THE TIMES CHELTENHAM FESTIVALS

LITERATURE 08

In association with

Waterstone's

Kate Adie
Simon Armitage
John Banville
Julian Fellowes
Michael Frayn
Patrick French
A C Grayling
Richard Holmes
Michael Holroyd
Sadie Jones
Penelope Lively
Andrew Motion
Alexander McCall Smith
Julia Neuberger
Ben Okri
D B C Pierre
Ian Rankin
Jeffrey Sachs
Anita Shreve
David Starkey
Kate Summerscale
Graham Swift
Fay Weldon
Timothy West

10 – 19 October
Box Office 0844 576 7979
cheltenhamfestivals.com

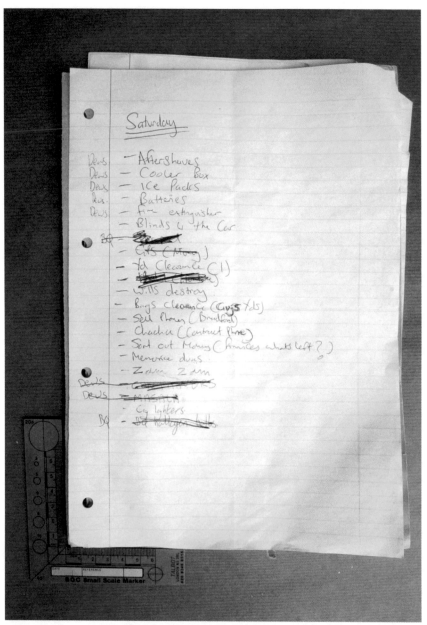

This unconventional 'shopping' list was found in a flat in Leeds rented by the London suicide bombers. Among the items listed were shrapnel (from B&Q), cigarette lighters and batteries.

THE ONE TRUE GOD, ALLAH

The rise of the British jihad

Richard Watson

On a warm April morning in 2004, I travelled out to Whitechapel in the East End of London to meet a young Englishman named Sulayman Keeler (formerly Simon Keeler) who was a recent convert to Islam. He was stocky with sharp eyes and a sparse, sandy beard, and was a leading member of the radical Islamist political group al-Muhajiroun, which translates from Arabic as 'the emigrants'. It was a group with a defined manifesto: fierce opposition to British foreign policy in Iraq and Afghanistan, the creation of a global Islamic state ruled by a caliph, and Islamic revolution in Britain, with the black flag of Islam being hoisted over 10 Downing Street.

Keeler and I sat and talked in a McDonald's for an hour about his beliefs and what had led to his conversion to Islam. 'It's like diving off the biggest diving board into the unknown,' he said. 'It's a complete shift from what I used to be. Before, I believed in democracy, freedom, and it was all about doing what I liked and making the most out of this life, enjoyment of it to the max, whereas when I embraced Islam all of that changed.'

He had grown up in the quiet Sussex town of Crawley. He was intelligent and articulate and spoke fluently, if rather predictably, about what he considered to be the decadence of Western society and about the atrocities he said had been perpetrated by Western states against Muslims across the world. For him, Islam was at war with the secular world. 'I don't believe in democracy,' he said. 'It's man-made. You're talking about a government that taxes the people to death. It oppresses many millions of people in the world. It wouldn't be such a shame to have them overturned.'

I had first begun to investigate al-Muhajiroun in the summer of 2001, shortly before the September 11 attacks in America. But my interest in the group had been rekindled by my experience of reporting in Iraq for BBC *Newsnight* in 2003. There I had witnessed the swift humiliation of Saddam Hussein's forces in Basra and had investigated his regime's torture and murder of Shi'a Muslims in the south of the country. Not a single Muslim I interviewed then expressed any regret about the fall of Saddam, yet during the months after my return to Britain, political Islamists from al-Muhajiroun had begun to use Britain's intervention in Iraq as a potent recruiting tool.

A couple of days after our meeting, I called Keeler to see if he would be interviewed for a film I was planning to make about al-Muhajiroun for the BBC. He asked me to meet him the following week at the Weavers' Fields community hall in Bethnal Green, east London. On arriving there I saw Keeler, sitting halfway back in a crowded room, with his young son next to him. The boy looked no more than five years old. At the very back, isolated from the men, was a small group of women, dressed in full-length *niqabs*; only their eyes were exposed.

'Today's topic, brothers, is knowledge,' announced the man with the microphone, standing at the front of the small hall. This was Abu Uzair, whose real name is Sajid Sharif; like many Islamist radicals he uses a nom de guerre taken from the Qur'an. The thirty-nine-year-old engineering graduate from Manchester continued: 'Look to capitalism, it has only existed for seventy-five years and it's

crumbling already. Communism is finished. The only other ideological belief around now, not a religion, Islam is not a religion... Let's make it clear: it's a political, ideological belief.'

Two video cameras on tripods were recording the speeches that night. A second man at the front, dressed in a long, white juba robe, took the microphone.

'When Tony Blair came out, George Bush came out at the same time and he said, "You're either with us or you're with the... terrorists." And what did we Muslims say?'

He paused for effect.

'We said, "We're not with you, we're with the...terrorists!"''

The crowd finished his sentence for him and cries of '*Allahu Akbar*' ('God is great') reverberated around the hall.

After breaking for prayers, Abu Uzair took the microphone once again.

'When they speak about September 11, when the two planes magnificently run through those buildings, people turn around and say, "Hang on a second, that is barbaric. Why did you have to do that?" You know why? Because of ignorance.'

At this point, I stood up and interrupted.

'You describe the 9/11 attacks, planes flying into the twin towers, and said it was magnificent, how can you justify that whether you're a Muslim, a Christian or a Jew?'

'For us it's retaliation,' Abu Uzair replied. 'Islam is not the starter of wars. If you start the war we won't turn the other cheek.'

'But the killing of innocent civilians can't be right?'

'It can't be right according to you,' he said, jabbing his finger at me. 'According to you, it can't be right. According to Islam, it's right. When you talk about innocent civilians, do you not kill innocent civilians in Iraq? Do you not kill innocent civilians indiscriminately in Afghanistan?'

'I wouldn't describe that as "magnificent",' I said.

'Islamically speaking, it's magnificent. I don't believe in democracy. From my perspective, it's a magnificent day in history

because it changed history.'

After the meeting ended, I asked Keeler whether he agreed that the September 11 attacks had been magnificent. 'You talk about 3,000 so-called innocents,' he said. 'What about the 200,000 innocents in Afghanistan? What about the one million children in Iraq who died as a result of America's foreign policy? Let's remember who we're talking about. You're crying about the fact that America, the oppressor, has been punched in the nose. That's what happened. You're talking about one man, Tony Blair, who sends a bunch of aircraft into Iraq, bombs a bunch of people. You're talking about another man, Osama bin Laden, who sends a bunch of aeroplanes into America and bombs a bunch of people – what is the difference? You tell me.'

The more time I spent with Keeler, the more I began to hear echoes of the anti-Western, revolutionary rhetoric preached by his mentor and leader, Omar Bakri Mohammed, the Islamist cleric who led al-Muhajiroun and has inspired many hundreds of young men to embrace radical Islam in Britain. He used to be dismissed as a fool and a crank by many in the British security and intelligence services, MI5 and MI6. But a large number of his recruits have received terrorist training in Pakistan and Afghanistan, and some have gone on to plan and carry out terrorist attacks. A week before my meeting with Keeler, officers from the Metropolitan Police's Anti-Terrorism Branch had arrested nine men in connection with a plot to blow up bars, nightclubs and the Bluewater shopping centre in Kent, England. The joint police and security service investigation had been code-named 'Operation Crevice' and it was the most complex counterterrorism investigation ever undertaken in Britain at that time. Half a ton of ammonium nitrate fertilizer, which can be used to make truck and car bombs, had been recovered from a lock-up in west London. The leader of the plot and two of his conspirators were, like Keeler, from Crawley, and had links with al-Muhajiroun and its leader.

Omar Bakri Mohammed was preaching hate in Britain for more

than twenty years, unencumbered by the state. A hard core of extremist radicals joined him, infecting generations of young British Muslims with their nihilistic interpretation of Islam. Jonathan Evans, director general of MI5 and the head of its counterterrorism since the September 11 attacks, has warned that the work of intelligence agencies alone will not be sufficient to defeat terrorism in Britain. He has concluded that, 'the violence directed against us is the product of a much wider extremist ideology, whose basic tenets are inimical to the tolerance and liberty which form the basis of our democracy'. But MI5's warning about the dangers posed by extremist ideology has come too late. Western democracies have been disastrously slow to recognize where the true battle lines were drawn. Back in the 1990s, the radicals preaching in London and other British cities, and the networks they were creating, were judged largely as a threat not to Britain but to countries overseas. An MI5 source told me that the service 'was just becoming aware of a significant acceleration in extremist Islamist activity' as late as 2003. By then, hundreds of British extremists had received terrorist training abroad and some were planning attacks on home soil. This was a 'failure of imagination' by the government and security services, says Sir Paul Lever, who used to chair the Joint Intelligence Committee. Another source responsible for synthesizing reports for the government told me that it was 'a massive intelligence failure' and that MI5 had been 'hugely complacent' about the threat from Islamists.

The complacency within the British establishment, in both the government and MI5, was shattered in London on the morning of July 7, 2005 when four young British Muslims murdered fifty-two of their fellow citizens. Since then huge resources have been diverted to MI5 in an effort to catch up with the scale of the threat. But much of the British state's response to the accelerating terror threat at home has concentrated on peripheral measures: robust counterterrorism laws; court orders against journalists, who are being forced to hand over their research; proposals to detain people without trial, first for ninety days and, most recently, a new law which makes forty-two

days' detention 'acceptable' in times of national crisis; increased surveillance with security cameras; the tracking of people's movements through the use of e-tickets such as the Oyster card on the London Underground. There is a sense that the state's grip is tightening.

Yet rather than being susceptible to these generalized responses, the terrorist threat posed by Muslim extremists is specific and predictable, with mappable links criss-crossing their way back to the early 1990s, when radical clerics were allowed to settle and work in Britain. If you track the connections, what emerges is how many of the plotters and perpetrators knew each other or were friends. This should make investigating terrorist plots easier than if they were the work of random and disconnected groups, but it also raises an important question: how did we arrive at this state of affairs?

This is the story of the British jihad.

ISLAMISM IN ENGLAND

Omar Bakri Mohammed was born in Aleppo, Syria, in 1958, and was recruited to the Muslim Brotherhood as a teenager.

Founded in Egypt in 1928 while the country was under British rule, the Muslim Brotherhood aimed to defeat the powers of colonialism and imperialism by creating unity among Arab states and introducing Islamic law. The Brotherhood was viewed as a major threat by regimes and dictatorships across the Arab world; it was a populist movement which could mobilize huge support and threaten secular nationalist leaders such as Gamal Abdel Nasser, President of Egypt from 1956 to 1970.

In repeated crackdowns, Egyptian secret police detained and tortured hundreds of Brotherhood members, including the movement's intellectual leader, Sayyid Qutb (1906–66), and Ayman al-Zawahiri, who would become Osama bin Laden's second-in-command. Born in a village in northern Egypt, Qutb's origins were humble but he was an intelligent child and by the age of ten had

learned to recite the Qur'an by rote, a prodigious feat of memory known as attaining hafiz. After university in Cairo and while he was still in his twenties, he published several influential books on the subject of the Islamic revival, the notion that Muslims must return to the pure, simple ways of the Prophet. Much of his philosophy was drawn from medieval Islamic scholars such as Ibn Taymiyyah. Qutb believed it was the duty of all Muslims to create an Islamic state governed only by the law of God.

After studying in America for two years, at Stanford University, Colorado State University and a teacher's college in Washington, DC, Qutb returned to Egypt in 1951, disgusted by what he considered to be the decadence and immorality of Western society. He said that Christian churches were no more than 'entertainment centres and sexual playgrounds'. He was even more critical of Muslims in his home country and, most trenchantly, of Nasser, whom he condemned for failing to institute sharia law. Consequently, Qutb believed that his fellow Muslims were in *jahiliyya*, an Islamic concept describing a state of wicked ignorance before the Qur'an was revealed to Mohammed in the seventh century AD, and that Western habits and influences were contaminating their faith. Qutb had no respect for secular Arab nationalism in Egypt or across the wider region. He believed that allegiance to country was in violation of the higher allegiance to God, and he wrote of fealty to the global Muslim community or umma. His revolutionary ideas were embraced by the Brotherhood, which plotted to murder the Egyptian president in the name of Allah. In 1954, the Brotherhood was implicated in a failed attempt on Nasser's life and the movement was banned. Six suspects were executed and thousands were rounded up and imprisoned, including Qutb, who received a fifteen-year sentence.

Qutb wrote his most celebrated book, *Milestones*, from his prison cell. This book remains an inspiration to the Sunni jihadists of al-Qaida. 'Those who say that Islamic Jihaad was merely for the defense of the "homeland of Islam' diminish the greatness of the Islamic way

of life," Qutb wrote, explaining that all systems which stand in the way of the creation of an Islamic state would have to be destroyed. 'If Islam is again to play the role of the leader of mankind, then it is necessary that the Muslim community be restored to its original form.'

He went on: 'Islam cannot accept or agree to a situation which is half Islam and half *jahiliyya*...The mixing and coexistence of the truth and falsehood is impossible. When the above mentioned obstacles and practical difficulties...are put in [Islam's] way, it has no recourse but to remove them by force.'

These were dangerous words and a direct threat to the secular Egyptian elite. Qutb was executed in Egypt in 1966 for plotting a coup from inside prison, and became a martyr for jihadists across the world. After Qutb's death, his brother, Mohammed, fled to Saudi Arabia, carrying his books and ideas with him. Osama bin Laden himself is reported to have attended Mohammed Qutb's lectures in the Kingdom.

Admirers of Sayyid Qutb describe him as an intellectual – a political Islamist, not a terrorist – and argue that his justification for violence must be understood in the context of the repression he experienced in Egypt. But there is a causal link between what he wrote and today's Islamic terrorists. Qutb combined political aspirations with a desire for a new fundamentalism that would sweep away the colonial influence in Arab lands as well as pan-Arab nationalism and communism in its wake. For Qutb's followers, such as Osama bin Laden and Ayman al-Zawahiri, there can be no accommodation between the righteous realm of Islam, *Dar ul-Islam*, and the land of hostility, or *Dar ul-Harb*. The idea of perpetual war in the name of Allah is fundamental to jihadi ideology and to understanding the motivations of al-Qaida's leaders in the tribal areas of the north-west frontier of Pakistan and Islamist extremists in cities across Britain.

Following Sayyid Qutb's execution, the Muslim Brotherhood faced brutal suppression across the Middle East. In Syria, it was

banned but continued as an underground movement, its members plotting to overthrow the ruling Ba'ath Party throughout the 1970s. There were sporadic crackdowns and expulsions. In 1977, at the peak of this struggle, Bakri Mohammed, then a nineteen-year-old member of the Brotherhood, was expelled from Syria for his political activities. He fled to Beirut in Lebanon, where he joined another Islamist movement, Hizb ut-Tahrir or 'the Party of Liberation'. Hizb ut-Tahrir's central aim was the creation of a single Islamic state in the Middle East – the *khilafah* or caliphate. Supporters mourn the year 1923, when Turkey's secular government, led by Mustafa Kemal Ataturk, overthrew the last caliph, who ruled the Ottoman Empire.

After two years in Lebanon, Bakri Mohammed travelled to Cairo, where he says he attended one of the world's most ancient universities, al-Azhar. He later told an Australian academic researcher that he was in conflict with his teachers there and soon left for Saudi Arabia to enrol at the Islamic School of al-Saltiyah in Mecca. Hizb ut-Tahrir was banned in Saudi Arabia, as it was in most countries in the Middle East, so Bakri Mohammed launched a new group in Jiddah on March 3, 1983 – the sixtieth anniversary of the fall of the Ottoman Empire. He called this group Jamaat al-Muhajiroun, the 'community of the emigrants', a reference to the followers of Mohammed in the Qur'an known as the *Sahaba*. The Saudi authorities soon suspected him of plotting against the ruling House of Sa'ud, which Bakri Mohammed regarded as *kufr*, or being without faith. His house was raided in March 1985 and the police found a proscribed book written by one of the leaders of Hizb ut-Tahrir. Bakri Mohammed says he was imprisoned and tortured before being expelled once more. He arrived in Britain as a political refugee on March 14, 1986. He cared nothing for Western democracy or for the country that had given him refuge; his first move, after settling in London, was to establish a UK branch of Hizb ut-Tahrir, a group with an established international network and reputation. He then began an aggressive recruitment campaign among the Muslim young of Britain.

Bakri Mohammed was a charismatic polemicist; in lectures and at meetings during the early 1990s he was even said to have called for the assassination of the then British prime minister, John Major, and later for the black flag of Islam to be hoisted over 10 Downing Street. Why was he permitted to continue preaching and agitating for violence against the British state?

The security services hugely underestimated the threat posed by political Islam within Britain. The rise of Islamic extremism in Algeria during the 1980s and early 1990s was monitored but considered an overseas phenomenon – the domain of MI6, not MI5, which concentrates on homeland security. As for Bakri Mohammed, he was dismissed as an eccentric buffoon, and yet even then, in the mid-1990s, long before the attacks of September 11 and the London bombings of July 7, he was engaged in creating a network of extremists and terrorist sympathizers among alienated British-born Muslims.

In some ways Bakri Mohammed faced greater opposition from within Hizb ut-Tahrir than from the British state; the group's powerful international leaders considered his work to be a distraction from their main objective: an Islamic revolution in the Middle East. 'Bakri didn't believe theologically in restricting the *khilafah* to the Arab countries of the Middle East: he wanted the *khilafah* in Britain,' says Rashad Ali, who, in 1994, as a fourteen-year-old in Sheffield, had fallen under the influence of Hizb ut-Tahrir after one of their members was invited to lecture at his school, Abbeydale Grange. Within a year of that lecture, Ali was a fully signed-up member of Hizb ut-Tahrir, organizing events for the party. He finally left after twelve years at the heart of the organization, and has since joined a number of senior defectors who have publicly criticized Hizb ut-Tahrir for secretly supporting the use of political violence to establish a global Islamic state. Hizb ut-Tahrir, however, denies this and claims to be a peaceful, political movement.

The conflict between Bakri Mohammed and the international leadership of Hizb ut-Tahrir led to his eventual expulsion from the

group in January 1996. Cast adrift once again, Bakri Mohammed and his closest followers set up al-Muhajiroun, in imitation of the small group he had founded in Saudi Arabia thirteen years earlier. The intention was to use al-Muhajiroun to recruit young ideologues committed to forming a caliphate in Britain. The timing was fortuitous. The civil war in the Balkans following the break-up of Yugoslavia was creating the circumstances for the radicalization of a generation of young British Muslims who were disturbed by the suffering of their fellow Muslims in Bosnia.

THE BOSNIAN JIHAD

Takbir!' shouts a bearded fighter, brandishing an AK-47 automatic assault rifle in the air, encouraging the small army of several thousand Muslim fighters gathered around him to reply.

'*Allahu Akbar!*' they shout in response.

The grainy video clips of Arab volunteer fighters gathering in Bosnia to confront the Serb opponents can still be found on the Internet today. For the price of a coach ticket, young British Muslims were able to travel to the Balkans to fight alongside these Arab volunteers, the mujahedin, who had arrived from Muslim lands in the early 1990s to support the Bosnian Muslim army as much as they could in its war against the Serbs. Hundreds of British Muslims joined the caravan. One such volunteer was Andrew Rowe, a Londoner with Jamaican parents who had converted to Islam at the age of nineteen. In July 1995 he was wounded by shrapnel when the convoy he was travelling in was attacked. He returned to England, his Bosnian adventure over. British Muslims such as Rowe, who had come back from fighting with the mujahedin, were received with respect in the radical Muslim community in Britain. From his base in London, Rowe continued to pursue jihad and in 1999 he attempted to travel to Georgia, carrying 12,000 US dollars, so as to be closer to the war in Chechnya, another site of conflict for the mujahedin. He claimed the money was for 'humanitarian assistance'. In 2005 he was

eventually convicted of plotting a terrorist attack after he was found in possession of training manuals giving instructions on how to fire 82mm mortars and coded messages about weapons and explosives. Deputy assistant commissioner Peter Clarke, head of the Metropolitan Police's Anti-Terror Branch, said Rowe was 'a global terrorist... A violent and dangerous man has been brought to justice.'

After an uneasy peace was reached in Bosnia in 1995, and the country was divided into separate Bosnian Muslim, Serbian and Croatian enclaves, Western intelligence officers set about gathering information on the mujahedin's international brigades. One intelligence report, filed by the Nato-led Stabilisation Force known as SFOR, concluded that units 'consisted of several hundred warriors. Some of them were also used as instructors in the Muslim Bosniac army.'

Corporal Jean-Philippe Lavigne, who filed that report, had been seconded to the US 629th Military Intelligence Battalion in Bosnia near the town of Zenica, where the mujahedin fighters had been based during the conflict. As well as gathering intelligence on their past activities, he observed how many had settled in the country, marrying local women and introducing a fierce, puritanical version of Islam to the region, in complete contrast to the mild, tolerant faith practised by most Bosnian Muslims (who tended to be ethnic Slavic converts) before the war. 'Strict Islamic law...began to govern affairs. Women there took to wearing veils and long black robes, and men had long beards. They didn't drink or smoke or speak to visitors,' he wrote.

In Britain, against the background of the Bosnian jihad, Bakri Mohammed began to tour towns and cities with large Muslim populations. There were frequent al-Muhajiroun meetings in London, Luton, Derby, Manchester and Crawley. It was in Crawley where he encountered a new recruit, a restless teenager named Omar Khyam. Khyam was not from a fundamentalist family: his uncle, who lived on the same street, was married to a white Christian woman and prided himself on his secularism. His father, who ran a

textile business from Karachi and Belgium, was absent for long periods of time but friends say his son appeared stable and happy at school where he was admired as an outstanding cricketer. Like many teenagers he enjoyed music and fast cars. But in the late 1990s his behaviour began to change. He fell under the influence of a group of radicals who prayed at his local mosque at Langley Green.

Khyam's family began to notice changes in him. He became far more interested in Islam and started praying five times a day and reading the Qur'an. This relatively privileged middle-class boy was becoming obsessed with Islamism and in particular with the conflict between Pakistan and India over the disputed Himalayan territory of Kashmir. As Khyam's uncle would tell me later, few in the community knew much, if anything, about radical political Islam at the time, and Bakri Mohammed fully exploited this ignorance. The radical cleric lectured at Khyam's youth club in Crawley and, in 1999, managed to get himself invited to lead the sixth-form assembly at Hazlewick School, where Khyam was a pupil. 'He did come into the school in the name of religious inclusion,' said Gordon Parry, the present head teacher, who taught there at the time. 'We didn't know about his background or views. No one really realized at the time. There was a kind of collective naivety about radical Islamic lecturers then.'

Some prominent members of Crawley's Muslim community were concerned about Bakri Mohammed's influence on boys. Khyam's uncle, Sajjad Ahmed, says the community tried to ban al-Muhajiroun from speaking at the Langley Green mosque and the youth club and attempted to stop the group distributing leaflets in the town. 'We did as much as we could,' he told me. 'They preyed on boys at the mosque and even in the shopping centres, getting them when they were young and impressionable. They showed them videos of the injustices Muslims were suffering, and then channelled their anger into hatred.'

In 1999, on a family holiday to Pakistan, Khyam met a representative of a terrorist group that trained fighters in Kashmir. He was inspired. He returned to Britain determined to help fight the

Indian army in Kashmir, and in January 2000 he told his mother he was going on an educational trip to France, then flew to Pakistan alone. Once there his old contacts proved invaluable. Travelling east from Islamabad into the foothills of the Himalayas, Khyam made his way to a camp in Pakistan-controlled Kashmir where he spent three months training with automatic weapons. He has said that Pakistan's intelligence service, the ISI, was providing much of the training, a credible claim supported by some inside the Ministry of Defence.

Back in Crawley, Khyam's family were making desperate attempts to locate him. His uncle sought a meeting with Bakri Mohammed to try to find out precisely where his nephew had gone. Bakri Mohammed denied any involvement, but said that if Khyam had left to train at a camp in Pakistan he should be 'praised for fulfilling his Islamic duty'; the family should be proud of his courage. In the end, through the family's contacts at Military Intelligence in Pakistan, Khyam was tracked down to the camp high in the mountains. Messages were relayed to his commanders and, eventually, the young recruit agreed to come down to meet his grandfather, who was waiting for him in the valley below. Khyam agreed to travel back to Britain where, to the surprise of much of the family, he received a hero's welcome, with supporters lining the hall of his house, showering him with flower petals as he walked in.

By now it was clear to all who knew him that Khyam, the boy who had supported Manchester United and wanted to play cricket for England, was in thrall to extreme political Islam. In an attempt to break its hold, his family persuaded him to return to full-time education. He was due to start a foundation course at London Metropolitan University in the autumn of 2001, but in the summer he travelled back to Pakistan again, ostensibly to attend a friend's wedding. Once there he slipped over the border into Afghanistan.

Shortly after Khyam had returned from Afghanistan I called his family to ask for an interview with him. They put me in contact with Khyam by phone. He told me that he had travelled 'all over Afghanistan', adding that 'the Taliban are the most hospitable people

in the world'. He estimated that there were 60,000 families from the Arabian peninsula living in Afghanistan and that Osama bin Laden had a firing range near the capital, Kabul. He refused to elaborate about the 'firing range' but he said it was easy for British recruits to get into Afghanistan. 'All you have to do is contact pro-Taliban groups in Pakistan,' he explained. 'They have stalls. You get in with them.' Four years later Khyam was arrested in a hotel room in Crawley as the prime suspect in a plot to blow up bars and nightclubs, including the Ministry of Sound in London, with a home-made fertilizer bomb.

THE WAR ON TERROR

On September 11, 2001 at 08.46.40 Eastern Standard Time, American Airlines Flight 11 crashed into the North Tower of the World Trade Center. Sixteen minutes and thirty-one seconds later, United Airlines Flight 175 was flown straight into the South Tower. These horrific attacks and their aftermath were captured on live television; for al-Qaida it was a huge propaganda coup. That night, in the Iqra Islamic centre in Beeston, Leeds, Mohammed Sidique Khan organized an unofficial party to celebrate the operation which had claimed 3,000 lives. The future leader of the London bombers was running community activities at the centre with extremist associates.

Nine days later, President George Bush addressed the Senate: 'Tonight, we are a country awakened to danger and called to defend freedom. Our grief has turned to anger and anger to resolution. Whether we bring our enemies to justice or bring justice to our enemies, justice will be done.'

The president's war on terror had begun.

Back in Britain analysts working in the Vauxhall Cross headquarters of Britain's Secret Intelligence Service, MI6, were re-examining every lead on Islamist extremism in their files. On mainland Europe there was a similar push for intelligence and soon evidence from recent counterterrorist operations was being

reassessed. Two days after the September 11 attacks, I flew to Milan to meet an Italian counterterrorism officer who had agreed to show me a terrorist safe house which had recently been raided by the police.

Driving in an unmarked car, we entered a shabby suburb on the outskirts of the city. The officer slowed down and pointed up at a dilapidated flat. When the Italian police had broken down the door they had found a document factory inside; forged passports, some incomplete, were scattered across the flat. There were lists of telephone numbers and motivational videos celebrating jihad.

I was told the flat had been secretly bugged before the police raid and the occupants, four Tunisian men led by a Sami Ben Khemais Essid, were recorded discussing explosives training they had received in Afghanistan and their support of the 'Sheikh', a reference to Osama bin Laden. Police believe they were planning to target the US Embassy in Rome. Ben Khemais Essid was known to be a supporter of a North African terror network. He was covertly tracked across Europe as he travelled by train to meet other cells of extremists in Germany and in Spain, where he visited a Syrian radical named Abu Dahdah. Both men were full of praise for a London-based cleric named Abu Qatada, whom they regarded as a spiritual leader. Other intelligence, this time from Germany, also pointed to the cleric's Europe-wide influence. In December 2000, German special forces had raided an apartment in Frankfurt. Inside they found bomb-making equipment, false identity papers and a video of what appeared to be a reconnaissance trip to the Christmas market in Strasbourg. The video recordings were made on December 23. Four men, led by Salim Boukari, were all later convicted of planning to bomb the market in Strasbourg. Prosecutors said three of the four men had spent time in Sheffield and London, planning and fund-raising for the attack. In February 2001, British counterterrorism police questioned Abu Qatada in connection with the Christmas market plot. He was in possession of £170,000 in cash and an envelope containing £805 marked 'For the mujahedin in Chechnya'. The Terrorism Act (2000) made it an offence if someone 'knows or

has reasonable cause to suspect that it [money] will or may be used for the purposes of terrorism'. Abu Qatada was questioned by the Metropolitan Police but released without charge in February 2001.

Like many Islamist radicals, Abu Qatada had found refuge in England in 1993 when he arrived from Jordan to claim asylum, which he was granted the following year. He would be joined in Britain by many other Islamic militants from Jordan, Saudi Arabia and the Maghrib. Some of these asylum seekers, especially those from North Africa, had previously been living in France but had left the country when the French authorities cracked down on Islamic militants after a bombing outrage on the Paris Metro on July 25, 1995 carried out by Algerians. The French intelligence service warned their British counterparts about the activities of Abu Qatada and other Islamists living in London. The French considered London – or 'Londonistan', as it became known – to be a safe haven for Islamic radicals, just as it had been for revolutionaries and anarchists in the nineteenth century. They were alarmed by the carelessness of the British security services, by how seemingly relaxed they were about the threat posed by radical Islam and by how porous the British borders were.

When I returned from Italy towards the end of September 2001, I wrote to Abu Qatada to request a meeting but received no reply. Neighbours said that he had left his house in Acton, west London, and had disappeared. I was told that he used to lecture after Friday prayers at a youth club called the Four Feathers, just north of the Marylebone Road in London, but when I turned up at the club the doors were chained shut. A note on the door explained that the club had been temporarily moved to an office building on the nearby Lisson Green estate.

A week or so later, on a cold autumn morning, I rode my motorbike on to the council estate and parked outside the ramshackle building that served as the youth centre's office. I was looking for a woman with grey hair in her sixties named Betty Muspratt, a youth worker who, I'd been told, had met Abu Qatada. She had worked on

the estate for thirteen years and, it seemed, knew everybody and everybody's secrets. She told me how she had met Abu Qatada in 1996 and how his lectures had quickly become popular. 'Between one hundred and one hundred and forty Muslims met at the Four Feathers club every Friday,' she said. 'The only time I saw Abu Qatada is when he came around with an interpreter to negotiate the rent – the club gets forty pounds a week for the prayer room so I thought, why not?'

Abu Qatada's followers revered him for his deep knowledge of jihadi theology. He told them that the mujahedin fighters are sacred to God. 'The role of mujahedin is dictated by what the prophet said: "Whoever fights to make the word of God supreme, then it is for the sake of God." Therefore, if the jihad is to make the word of God supreme, this is what we call the Islamic Jihad.' In an interview he gave to the Canadian Broadcasting Corporation, he said, 'No doubt that human life is based on conflict. This is what we see today and is confirmed by the conflicts which arose between sects, countries and groups. No rights or principles can be respected, accepted or imposed except through the use of force.'

Extremists from across Europe visited the Lisson Green estate to hear Abu Qatada speak. Djamel Beghal, Kamel Daoudi, Nizar Trabelsi and Jerome Courtailler, who would each be convicted of terrorism offences, were all known to have met the cleric. The so-called twentieth hijacker in the September 11 attacks, Zacarias Moussaoui, knew Abu Qatada well and is believed to have attended Friday prayers at Lisson Green. Audio tapes of Abu Qatada's sermons were found in the Hamburg flat of Mohammed Atta, the September 11 terrorist leader.

Abu Qatada's teachings, in the incongruous surroundings of an inner-city youth club, were in direct support of terrorism overseas and MI5 was aware of this. Betty Muspratt told me that police officers approached her as early as 1999 to ask if a covert camera could be installed at the Four Feathers club to record Abu Qatada's meetings. It is not clear whether this camera was ever fitted, but an

intelligence analyst, who spoke to me on condition of anonymity, was shown a video recording of Abu Qatada addressing a group of twelve followers in London in 2001, before the September 11 attacks. His disciples, sitting around him in a dimly lit room, ask about jihad and suicide attacks. Abu Qatada replies that such acts are permissible and that paradise is waiting. 'I can smell paradise in the air,' he says. Comments such as this and his alleged links to European terrorist cells led Spain's leading counterterrorism judge, Baltasar Garzon, to name Abu Qatada as the 'spiritual leader of the mujahedin in Europe', an accusation denied by the cleric.

Abu Qatada is an exponent of a violent Islamic doctrine known as *takfirism*. Followers, known as *takfiris*, believe that it is religiously permissible to punish other Muslims who oppose an Islamic revival. They take the arrogant and deadly view that Muslims who oppose them are also opposing the will of God. Those who oppose the will of God render themselves apostates, and the penalty for apostasy is death. This is the doctrine of *takfir* as introduced to modern Islamic thought by Sayyid Qutb.

'No doubt that the Qur'an, the Sunna and the life of the Prophet order the Muslim to carry on jihad and fighting,' Abu Qatada has said. 'This is something no Muslim can deny. Any Sheikh who tries to deny it or strip it of its real meaning is considered an act of apostasy. No doubt human life is based on conflict...no rights or principles can be respected, accepted or imposed except through the use of force.'

Three months after my first meeting with Betty Muspratt, I returned to Lisson Green. This was in December 2001 and US forces had just defeated the Taliban in Afghanistan. I had been invited to watch and film youth-club rappers who met every week in a community hall. A young black teenager held the microphone aloft, swaggering across the makeshift stage: 'My name is MC Jetski and I'm MC-ing for the Taliban Crew. Because of the war, yeah, we're all Muslims.'

Preparations for war: the living room of the rented flat in Leeds where the July 7 bombers prepared for their suicide mission on the London Underground

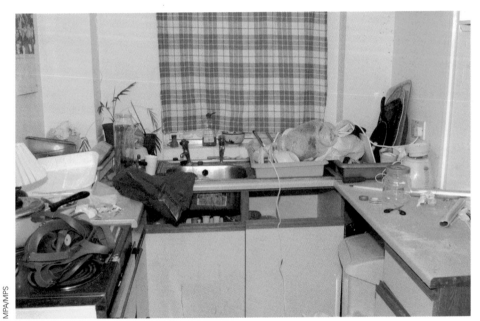

The bomb-makers used gas masks when boiling hydrogen peroxide, a key ingredient in the explosive devices that were used to murder fifty-two people

The bombs were made using equipment easily available from local hardware stores

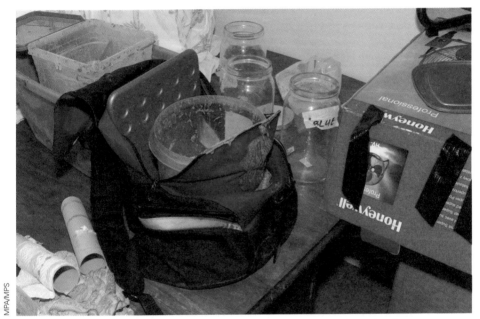

Residue of explosive material, made from mixing triacetone triperoxide and masala spice

This was more than teenage bluster. Over the preceding two years radical Islam had swept through the estate. At its peak, in 1999, around fifty teenagers living in Lisson Green converted to Islam. Some other children who were already Muslim suddenly became far more devout. Certainly Betty Muspratt noticed a change. She said that most parents were pleased their children were staying away from crime and drugs. Islam, it seemed, offered new direction. 'I just felt they were so positive,' she said. 'They showed respect with heads held high.'

What the relieved parents did not know was that the boys were being converted by a 'messiah-like' figure who had returned to the estate after serving time in prison. This man, of North African origin, was known as Michael Jean-Pierre (it is not clear if this was his real name) and had fought in Bosnia with the mujahedin. He had returned home with shrapnel in his leg and began grooming teenagers on the estate by introducing them to radical Islam. Soon there was talk among these young converts of travelling abroad to deepen their knowledge of Islam.

One afternoon I sat in the kitchen of a small flat in Lisson Green and listened to an energetic, determined Eritrean Christian mother named Fifi Walker explain how extremism had affected her life. Her two sons, Hosea and Malaky, had converted to Islam in 1999. Soon afterwards they told their mother that they were dropping out of school to travel to Yemen. By the spring of 2000, fifteen-year-old Hosea and seventeen-year-old Malaky were studying at a madrasa 200 kilometres north of the Yemeni capital, Sanaa, close to the border with Saudi Arabia. They had travelled with three other boys from the estate, stopping off in Saudi Arabia on the way. Their air tickets were paid for by a mysterious Muslim benefactor and visas had been arranged. Just a couple of weeks after arriving at the school, Hosea was shot dead.

The family was told it was a tragic accident. One of the group of boys who had gone from Lisson Green to Yemen had apparently bought a gun from a local market and had accidentally discharged

the weapon while he was cleaning it. Hosea, who was sitting next to him, was fatally wounded in the chest. His death prompted the British Ambassador in Yemen, Victor Henderson, to make his own enquiries. He discovered that there were thirty British pupils at the madrasa. Hosea's family believe to this day that he would not have agreed to train for jihad and deny any suggestions that he might have received arms training. They say he was simply studying Arabic, but when I started to check the details of this story I came across evidence that supports the notion that the school was encouraging extremism.

American intelligence reports suggest that the head of the madrasa where Hosea studied was a fundamentalist cleric named Sheikh Muqbil al-Wadii. Evidence given during military hearings at the US detention centre in Guantánamo Bay puts forward the possibility that three 'enemy combatants' had passed through Sheikh Muqbil's hands in Yemen. The American intelligence reports allege that he funded trips to Pakistan and Afghanistan, where his young protégés trained in al-Qaida camps.

Other boys from the Lisson Green estate who travelled to Yemen also came under the influence of terrorist sympathizers. Richard Belmar, a big St Lucian lad who had grown up with Hosea and Malaky, travelled to Kandahár in Afghanistan in July 2001. He was later captured and taken to Guantánamo Bay as an 'enemy combatant'. Belmar told a US military tribunal that he had been trained at a terrorist camp in Afghanistan and attended public meetings led by the emir of al-Qaida, Osama bin Laden. He had been at lectures in London given by Abu Qatada at the Four Feathers youth club.

So the question has to be asked again: why were Abu Qatada and others like him allowed to live and preach in London? The answer lies in the attitude of the security services throughout the 1990s, right up to 2003. One intelligence analyst I spoke to told me that security officials had been hoping to garner intelligence from Abu Qatada and other radicals in exchange for allowing them the right to live in

Britain. It ended up being a very one-sided deal. In the opinion of the analyst I spoke to, Abu Qatada 'turned the whole of Europe into a recruiting ground for terror' while offering very little to the Security Service in return. It is also possible that MI5 was being given false information by their agents inside the jihadi networks. I have spoken to a senior Muslim leader who fears there may be individuals within the police, and perhaps even MI5, working as agents of influence on behalf of the jihadists. The community elder I spoke to (whose identity I have agreed to protect) told me that following a confidential meeting with police, during which he named extremists operating in his town, one of those he identified had threatened him and warned him not to speak to the police again. The elder believes he was betrayed.

For an insider's view on how much the Security Service knew, I turned to Sir David Omand, who was appointed the British government's intelligence coordinator in 2002. Sir David is a former head of the Government Communications Headquarters, the interception and analysis centre in Cheltenham known as GCHQ. He says the radicalization of British Muslims was being 'observed and monitored' by the security authorities before the September 11 attacks. 'This phenomenon was certainly not missed by the UK authorities, although being able to prove that a criminal offence against UK law, as it then stood, was being planned was obviously tricky in relation to most of the propaganda and collection of funds [through registered charities]. The important point is that security authority monitoring of this activity did not reveal intentions to direct violence in the UK or at UK interests overseas.'

It seems there was an unwritten agreement that Islamist radicals could operate freely in Britain so long as their activities were concentrated abroad. British authorities were effectively relying on an Islamic concept called the Covenant of Security under which, according to Islamic law, Muslims should never attack their hosts unless they themselves are under attack. The assumption that this

covenant would protect British interests at home allowed the extremist clerics to operate without restriction from the British state.

THE PAKISTAN CONNECTION

In February 2001, seven months before the September 11 attacks, a heavy-set man with a checked Saudi scarf over his face stood on a grass verge outside a commercial office building in Tottenham, north London, which served as the British headquarters of al-Muhajiroun. 'My name is Izzadeen and I am from London,' he said. 'There is a growing surge among Muslim communities inside the UK that stretches from Bradford all the way down to London,' he continued. 'Muslims are recognizing their responsibility towards Muslims outside, whether that be inside Kashmir or inside Chechnya or inside Saudi Arabia. Recruitment is taking place in many mosques and many are coming forward to train for jihad.'

Three other jihadists standing next to him, their faces concealed like his, nodded in approval. Izzadeen Abdullah, a convert to Islam, said that training Islamist radicals for jihad was already well under way in Britain. 'Muslims inside the UK will train physically, they will do some navigational skills, they will do some patrolling skills and they will do some ambushing skills – they will do skills needed for jihad but without weapons. But for training that fulfils the obligation – because we are talking of something that is prescribed by Islam – they must go abroad and train with weapons.'

Izzadeen was raised in east London, the son of Christian Jamaican parents. After converting to Islam at the age of seventeen, he left Britain to live in Pakistan and Kashmir, where he spent seven months training with weapons. If Omar Bakri Mohammed and Abu Qatada were the first generation of terrorist sympathizers and propagandists to recruit in Britain, young men such as Izzadeen were the next. 'There are some Muslims who go to America because light arms are available there,' he told me. 'But why not take the opportunity to use the heart of the enemy that is attacking us?'

At the time of our meeting, two organizations were offering military-style training to supporters of al-Muhajiroun. A company called Sakina Security Services was advertising 'the ultimate jihad challenge', a course in firearms training in the American state of Alabama. Another group, based at the Finsbury Park mosque in north London under the leadership of the radical cleric Abu Hamza, was offering training at a camp deep in the Oregon backcountry, near the farming community of Bly. MI5 would have known about plans to send British citizens abroad for arms training – Hamza's organization openly advertised on the Internet – yet no action was taken beyond maintaining the existing policy of watch and wait.

By the time I met Izzadeen, al-Muhajiroun had established a base in New York – its first overseas branch. Supporters would congregate at the Masjid al-Fatima mosque in Queens, which, in the mid-1990s, had been taken over by radicals from Hizb ut-Tahrir. New York quickly became an important centre of political work for al-Muhajiroun, but it was Pakistan that was central to the group's international plans. For its leader Bakri Mohammed the country held numerous attractions. A large network of fundamentalist madrasas was already in place; many of the most radical had been supported by the CIA during the 1980s, when Muslim fundamentalism was used as a powerful force to be deployed against the Soviet army in Afghanistan. These schools, and the training camps associated with them, provided a regular flow of fighters for the mujahedin. Bakri Mohammed believed these same networks could be exploited to provide training for al-Muhajiroun's members, who could also count on the support of some radical elements within Pakistan's intelligence service, the ISI, which had a long history of training the volunteers to fight in Afghanistan and Kashmir. Lastly, but perhaps most significantly, Pakistan was a nuclear power.

On November 24, 1999 Bakri Mohammed sent some of his most trusted aides to Lahore to launch the Pakistan branch of al-Muhajiroun. They held a press conference in the city to mark the event. Izzadeen was there, as was Abu Uzair, the man whom I would

film five years later describing the terrorist attacks on the twin towers as 'magnificent'. These pioneers were soon joined by two brothers from England, Adeel and Sajeel Shahid, who set up an office in Lahore in a single-storey, modern house at 101 Aurangzeb Block in New Garden Town. This address, with its neat lawn and shrubs outside, was the first place of arrival for a procession of young, committed jihadists who began to arrive from Britain.

Sajeel Shahid, a science graduate from the University of Manchester Institute of Science and Technology, was the more charismatic of the two brothers. Shahid has always denied involvement in extremism, but it is known that he took over the leadership of al-Muhajiroun in Pakistan and soon befriended a well-known Islamist named Khalid Khawaja, who worked for the ISI and claimed to be 'a personal friend' of Osama bin Laden.

With a support network in place, even more jihadi recruits began to arrive from Britain. In December 2000 a young Muslim from Birmingham named Bilal Mohammed travelled to Pakistan and made contact with al-Muhajiroun. He was recruited by extremists from the Pakistani group Jaish e-Mohammed and was trained to use explosives. On Christmas Day 2000 Bilal Mohammed became Britain's first Islamic suicide bomber when he put on an explosive vest and blew himself up outside an Indian army barracks in Kashmir, killing six soldiers and three local students in the blast. In Pakistan he was feted by Jaish e-Mohammed leaders as a martyr, while in Britain al-Muhajiroun proudly claimed him as one of their own.

One week after the September 11 attacks an American-Pakistani student named Mohammed Iqbal, a recruit from the New York branch of al-Muhajiroun, set off for Pakistan. First he flew to London, where he stayed with supporters of al-Muhajiroun and attended an Islamist rally outside the Pakistan High Commission in Lowndes Square. He eventually arrived in Lahore in the last week of September 2001 and moved into a house occupied by a British jihadi from Manchester named Hassan Butt. Born in Luton in 1980, Butt became involved in Islamist politics at the age of sixteen. Following

his expulsion from Wolverhampton University for Islamist activity, he was part of the vanguard who had arrived in Pakistan from Britain to help set up the al-Muhajiroun operation. He was valued as an excellent organizer and fund-raiser. (He would later publicly renounce his commitment to radical Islam.)

On October 7, American bombers attacked Afghanistan from bases in the Persian Gulf and from Diego Garcia, the British-controlled island in the Indian Ocean. US Special Forces moved into the country to coordinate fighters from the Northern Alliance, which opposed the Taliban. After less than five weeks of battle, Mullah Omar's Taliban theocracy was ousted from Kabul, but this humiliation served only to intensify the commitment of the British jihadis.

One young British volunteer who travelled to Pakistan was Kazi Rahman, who would be convicted in London in 2006 of trying to buy sub-machine guns from an undercover police officer at a motorway service station. In October 2001 he arrived in Lahore and went straight to al-Muhajiroun's office, where he was given money and assistance to cross the border into Afghanistan to fight with the Taliban. A source close to al-Muhajiroun told me how he had bought weapons from another British jihadi, Omar Sheikh, who was later indicted for kidnapping and murdering the American journalist Daniel Pearl. Omar Sheikh had become radicalized while studying at the London School of Economics and had direct contacts with al-Qaida in Pakistan.

In the weeks after the coalition attack on Afghanistan, a Canadian journalist named Anne Barnard met Mohammed Iqbal and Hassan Butt in a hotel lobby in Islamabad. They were with a man who was British and gave his name as Abdul Momin, almost certainly a pseudonym. Iqbal told Barnard that he felt 'absolutely no remorse' about the September 11 attacks. 'I saw the towers collapse but felt nothing for the Americans inside. I may hold an American passport, but I am not an American. I am a Muslim... I'm willing to kill the Americans. I will kill every American that I see in Afghanistan. And I'll kill every American soldier that I see in Pakistan.'

Hassan Butt claimed that one hundred foreign fighters had come to Pakistan to fight alongside the Taliban – at least sixty of them from Britain. Two recruits from Luton, Afzal Munir and Aftab Manzoor, both aged twenty-five, died in bombing raids on Kabul. A third Briton, Yasir Khan, from Crawley, was also killed in the raids. But Hassan Butt, who had taken on the role of media spokesman for al-Muhajiroun in Pakistan, praised their bravery. 'We are very envious, very happy for these people who have become martyrs,' he said. 'We too would like to be like this because to live and die for Islam is every Muslim's role in life.'

In spite of the deaths the number of recruits from Britain continued to grow. On October 4, 2001 Waheed Mahmood from Crawley left his job with British Telecom; he said he was on his way to attend a wedding in Pakistan. In fact, once in Pakistan he met Hassan Butt in Lahore and stayed on in the city, living in his flat there, the latest recruit to jihad.

In the period following the September 11 attacks, other British jihadists arrived in Pakistan's major cities. What they needed, however, was a way to get out to the North-west Frontier Province and to establish contact with al-Qaida and the remnants of the Taliban regime. A government-controlled computer company was to provide the perfect cover. On November 14, 2001 the Pakistan Software Export Board (PSEB) appointed a new managing director from Britain. His name was Sohail Shahid and he was the elder brother of Sajeel and Adeel, the two men who had set up al-Muhajiroun's office in Pakistan. Al-Muhajiroun viewed this as a master stroke, because the software company's government status could now be exploited for jihad. The PSEB had a network of guest houses across the country, so accommodation was no longer a problem for volunteers arriving from Britain, and the company had unparalleled access to advanced computers and websites, which were vital for disseminating al-Muhajiroun's propaganda. It also had access to official government papers and passes, which would guarantee safe passage through army checkpoints, even into remote

areas in the North-west Frontier Province.

While his older brother was in charge, Sajeel Shahid, al-Muhajiroun's local leader, was given a twelve-month consultancy agreement with the PSEB. Hassan Butt remembers how 'Sajeel would come into the offices dressed like the Taliban, whereas everyone else agreed to trim their beards and wear Western clothes to be discreet.' He says that the PSEB was being 'flooded' with al-Muhajiroun supporters.

The American jihadist Mohammed Iqbal was given a job with the software company and, conveniently, was posted to Peshawar, close to the border with Afghanistan. He was responsible for setting up a new technology park, but he seldom turned up for work. He later admitted to forging PSEB government passes to allow his jihadi contacts to move around Pakistan. Three government laptop computers he stole ended up in the hands of terrorists and his business card was found on what was left of the body of a suicide bomber who had blown himself up in Karachi.

There was growing disquiet in Pakistan about how the PSEB was being managed. In April 2002, Pakistan's Auditor General conducted an investigation into the company and concluded that there were serious financial irregularities. Sohail Shahid was forced out, though he says he did nothing wrong. When I spoke to him in 2006 I asked him if the PSEB had been run for the benefit of jihadis. He said no. 'I pushed from the start to keep anybody from al-Muhajiroun away from the company,' he said. He left the organization at the end of the 2002, as did Iqbal and other staff connected to al-Muhajiroun.

Al-Muhajiroun may have lost its government cover, but its support structure for jihad was by now well established. Hassan Butt says that at least 200 British citizens passed through the Pakistan network. While some were naive dreamers, others had murderous intent. Two of Bakri Mohammed's recruits, Asif Hanif and Omar Sharif, arrived in the Israeli city of Tel Aviv on April 30, 2003. They paused outside Mike's Place, a popular seafront music bar. If anyone had been watching closely, what happened next was a sure sign of an

attack. They dropped their passports and wallets into a skip and walked towards the main door. Twenty-one-year-old Hanif, described by friends at Southall mosque in west London as a 'gentle giant', detonated his suicide belt as a security guard tried to stop them going inside. The explosion ripped through the bar; three people died. Sharif's belt failed to explode and he fled the scene; his dead body was found in the sea several days later.

Both Hanif and Sharif had been supporters of al-Muhajiroun. They attacked Israel in the name of the Palestinian group Hamas, but their radicalization can be traced back to the summer of 2001, before the September 11 attacks, when they were in contact with Mohammed Sidique Khan, the future leader of the London bombers.

THE COVENANT IS BROKEN

During his time with the Pakistan Software Export Board, Mohammed Iqbal was free to roam the North-west Frontier Province. Looking across towards the Khyber Pass and Jalálábád beyond, he was frustrated by the success of Operation Enduring Freedom, which had forced the Taliban from power in Afghanistan. The training camps were closed and many of their allies were dead or in hiding. No longer could would-be jihadists visit Afghanistan to be trained in terrorist camps and al-Muhajiroun needed to find a way of training jihadists at new camps in the mountains of Pakistan.

In February 2003 Iqbal travelled across the North-west Frontier Province for five days with Sajeel Shahid, al-Muhajiroun's leader in Pakistan. They were looking for land where they would be free to train with guns and explosives. They found what they thought was the perfect area, high up in the mountains, several hours' walk from the road. A local religious leader agreed to help arrange training with arms. The two men returned to Peshawar excited at having found the location for a new training camp.

In the following weeks, British jihadis in Pakistan whiled away the dead hours in coffee bars. They felt they had reached an impasse.

With coalition forces firmly in control in Afghanistan, they questioned the purpose of launching suicide missions across the border. Many international fighters from al-Qaida had already died; al-Muhajiroun recruits had lost their lives as well. They firmly believed these men were martyrs – each one had become a *shaheed* – but the wider political goal to eject the infidel from Muslim lands, to create support for a caliphate, was no further forward. At a country house at Gujar Khan, near Rawalpindi, which had been built by Waheed Mahmood from Crawley, they began to discuss something entirely new and daring – mounting attacks on Britain from within Britain. What we need to do, Omar Khyam told his friends, 'is to hit the UK,' especially 'pubs, nightclubs and trains'.

Shortly after the meeting at Gujar Khan, many members of the al-Muhajiroun network returned to Britain, where they set about raising funds for further training in Pakistan. They held a barbecue in the garden of a house in Colindale, north London, occupied by Zaheer Ali, an al-Muhajiroun leader. The party – the jihadi equivalent of a charity dinner – went on long into the night. Several groups of committed extremists came together here. There were the 'Crawley Boys' – Omar Khyam, Waheed Mahmood and Jawad Akbar; the 'East London Crew', led by Anthony Garcia; and a group called the 'Luton Boys'. Hassan Butt, who had driven down from Manchester in his brother's sports car, was also present. Large tins for donations were passed around, and these were filled with banknotes amounting to many hundreds of pounds.

Precisely how much MI5 knew about what was going on is unclear. But I do know that MI5 was aware of the Luton cell as early as March 2003. Surveillance officers were also watching a Bedfordshire taxi driver they had code-named 'Bashful Dwarf'. He was under investigation for supplying money and equipment, such as night-vision glasses and camping gear, to al-Qaida operatives in Pakistan and was suspected of using human couriers to transport the goods abroad. MI5 also had, on file, the details of a telephone call he had made to someone named 'Siddeque Khan' [*sic*] in Beeston,

Yorkshire. We now know that this was Mohammed Sidique Khan, the leader of the London bombers. MI5 said later that neither of these men was considered a direct threat to Britain at the time because the focus of their activities and schemes seemed to be in Pakistan.

On May 6, 2003 Omar Khyam flew to Pakistan once again. As he entered the country he was photographed by the computerized immigration system PISCES, which had been paid for by the Americans to help Pakistan fight the president's war on terror. Khyam drove to Kohát, in the North-west Frontier Province, to attend a training camp where recruits learned how to make the poison ricin by grinding castor oil beans and how to make crude but deadly home-made explosives by mixing ammonium nitrate fertilizer with aluminium powder. These were available in local markets and could be bought without arousing suspicion. A test explosion in a mountain river near Kohát created a huge fountain of water. Fertilizer bombs had proved lethal in the past: a one-tonne IRA truck bomb had devastated the City of London on April 24, 1993 and in April 1995 Timothy McVeigh used a similar device to bomb the Alfred P. Murrah Federal building in Oklahoma City, killing 168 people.

After completing the explosives course in Kohát, Omar Khyam joined Anthony Garcia, from London, and Jawad Akbar, from Crawley, for the journey to another camp near the border with Kashmir. To avoid detection they first took a detour up the beautiful Swat valley, posing as Western tourists, before moving on to the camp. As arranged, other British jihadists joined them there. Among them was Sidique Khan, who arrived in Pakistan together with a friend from Leeds, on July 25. They were met at Islamabad Airport and travelled to the camp by truck. Once there, they all practised firing automatic rifles and rocket-propelled grenades (RPGs). Khyam took people aside at the camp to speak to them privately about their willingness to take part in a suicide mission. He also went with Sidique Khan and Anthony Garcia to a remote part of the camp to detonate half a kilogram of explosive they had made from mixing ammonium nitrate

and powdered aluminium, ingredients bought from a local market. The small charge was placed in a plastic bottle and, recklessly, the fuse was lit by hand. The explosion created a U-shaped hole in the ground.

By November 2003, Sidique Khan and Omar Khyam had returned to Britain. Sidique Khan was back at work as a teaching assistant in Leeds, while Khyam began to gather a bombing team around him. Anthony Garcia was instructed to buy 600 kilograms of ammonium nitrate fertilizer, which was placed in a self-storage lock-up in west London, just off the A4. Sealed sachets of aluminium powder were hidden in an old biscuit tin in Khyam's garden in Crawley. The plan to bomb targets in England was live.

OPERATION CREVICE

MI5 continued to watch 'Bashful Dwarf'. There were taps on his telephone and he was observed meeting numerous contacts, including Omar Khyam in London. This prompted MI5 to categorize Khyam as an essential target for surveillance. On another occasion surveillance officers followed a vehicle north up the M1. In the car were two unidentified suspects who were known to have been in contact with 'Bashful Dwarf'. MI5 was watching as the driver dropped his passenger off in Leeds before making the short journey south to Dewsbury where, in surveillance officers' language, he was 'housed' at his home address. This man was in fact Mohammed Sidique Khan – MI5 officers had just followed the future leader of the London bombers home.

Across the Atlantic, at the National Security Agency's vast information factory at Fort Meade, near Washington, DC, arrays of supercomputers were, as usual, sifting through billions of global telephone calls and emails. On, or around, February 6, 2004 an electronic communication was intercepted between Omar Khyam in Britain and Salahuddin Amin in Pakistan. The intercept was so alarming that American security officers immediately contacted their counterparts in Britain. In the intercepted message, Khyam had

asked about the correct ratios of ammonium nitrate fertilizer to aluminium powder necessary to make a viable bomb. His request prompted an urgent reassessment of MI5's investigation into both 'Bashful Dwarf' and Khyam. Prime Minister Tony Blair was informed via the Joint Intelligence Committee. What had been an inquiry into a plot to provide material assistance to al-Qaida overseas now turned into a race to stop a terrorist attack on British soil. MI5 was sure that Khyam had the intent and capability to strike. All available resources were diverted into a huge counterterrorism operation, code-named Operation Crevice, run by MI5 and the Metropolitan Police Anti-Terrorism Branch. It became the biggest surveillance operation ever undertaken in Britain, during which ninety-seven telephone lines were tapped and 34,000 hours of surveillance material were gathered. For the commander of the Metropolitan Police, Sir John Stephens, 'the great decision was how long to let it run and that's when the police and the Security Service lose sleep. Because you want to get evidence you try and run it as long as you possibly can to get that evidence.'

On February 20, MI5 officers secretly recorded Omar Khyam at home talking to another man about obtaining detonators for a bomb. Coincidentally, on the same day, a member of staff at Access Self Storage telephoned the police to report his suspicions about the contents of the lock-up. Counterterrorist police officers arrived the next morning and, on finding the 600-kilogram bag of fertilizer, took samples for laboratory analysis. The ammonium nitrate explosive was switched for an identical-looking inert substance and surveillance cameras were installed in the lock-up to catch the conspirators when they returned.

Elsewhere the surveillance operation continued, occupying hundreds of officers from the police and MI5. They were watching and listening once again as Khyam met Sidique Khan and the two men were heard discussing whether to say goodbye to their families. In one of the recorded exchanges there were clear indications of which man held the higher rank:

Khan: 'Are you really a terrorist?'
Khyam: 'They're working with us.'
Khan: 'You're serious?'
Khyam: 'No, I'm not a terrorist but they're working through us.'
Khan: 'There's no one higher than you.'

It is clear at this time that Khyam, the aspiring county cricketer from Crawley, was firmly in charge. Sidique Khan respected him as his leader, known in jihadi circles as an 'emir'.

In counterterrorism operations such as this there is always a tension between the desire to gather more evidence by letting the plot run and preserving public safety by making arrests. Two weeks after Khyam and Sidique Khan had met, the dangers of misjudging this balance were plain to see. In Spain, on March 11, 2004, a terrorist cell remotely detonated three bombs on a packed early-morning commuter train as it pulled into Atocha station in Madrid. Over the next three minutes another seven bombs exploded on three other trains, injuring almost 2,000 people and leaving 191 dead. The fertilizer-bomb plotters were overheard celebrating the attacks.

'Spain was such a beautiful job wasn't it, absolutely beautiful man, so much impact,' Waheed Mahmood said.

As pictures of the devastation at Atocha station were broadcast across the world, the consequences of losing control of Operation Crevice in Britain were clear. What if the conspirators had another stash of fertilizer in an unknown location? Could a second bomb be ready to be deployed?

Four days after the Madrid attacks, the waiting game was rewarded. Surveillance cameras recorded Khyam returning to Access Self Storage to inspect the 600-kilogram fertilizer bag. He chatted casually to a new female member of staff at the front desk, explaining to her that this would be the last month he would need storage. She was an undercover officer from MI5. Later, conversations secretly recorded in cars and houses suggested an attack was close. Surveillance officers overheard Khyam's fellow conspirator Waheed Mahmood discussing how to bring the plan

forward. 'Is it worth getting all the brothers together tonight and asking who would be ready to go? A little explosion at Bluewater [the shopping centre in Kent] tomorrow if you want... We haven't tested it but we could do one tomorrow.'

In another conversation, Khyam instructed the others on how to maximize the impact of an attack. 'It has to be big, yeah, it has to be destructive and everything. That's one. And second it has to be combined with something to make proper effect and terror.'

The conspirators were discussing attacking utilities.

'It has to be a simultaneous thing. The electric goes up, so it's a blackout. Then the gas lot move in and bang! Then the water – something goes on with the water. It's a simultaneous attack.'

By the end of March, the Metropolitan Police decided they could wait no longer. In Britain, armed officers carried out simultaneous raids, shortly after six on the morning of April 30. They arrested Omar Khyam, Waheed Mahmood and Jawad Akbar in Crawley, and Anthony Garcia in London, on suspicion of planning a terrorist attack.

At first, Khyam's family supported him. His uncle Ansar Khan said that there was 'absolutely no truth' in the allegations. 'These boys are the cricketers, they're Manchester United fans. Fish and chips is their favourite food.'

Mohammed Iqbal flew back from Pakistan to New York. Four days later he too was arrested and agreed to testify against the conspirators. He had been with Khyam and the other plotters every step of the way. In Britain, everything was now set for a successful trial, during which it would become clear that the police and intelligence services had prevented a major terrorist attack.

THE LONDON BOMBINGS

In the weeks after the fertilizer-bomb plotters were arrested, there were signs that Sidique Khan was becoming anxious. He telephoned a relative of Khyam to ask him, guardedly, for news.

Sidique Khan was reluctant to speak on the telephone and requested to meet him. The two men agreed to meet on the seafront in Grimsby. Sidique Khan was trying to find out whether the police or MI5 had been asking questions about Khyam's wider circle of contacts. He knew that his phone number was on Khyam's mobile phone, which the police had. In fact, Sidique Khan had less to worry about than he may have feared.

After Khyam's arrest, MI5 assessed all of his contacts, including Sidique Khan, dividing them into essential and desirable targets. The future leader of the London bombers was categorized as desirable but not essential; he was not placed under surveillance or investigated intensively because resources were already stretched. To MI5, he was a peripheral figure, a petty fraudster who might be interested in jihad abroad but who was not judged to be an imminent threat.

MI5 operatives had bugged and trailed Sidique Khan when he was with Omar Khyam on at least four occasions in February and March 2004. At the time, it is said, MI5 did not know Sidique Khan's real name, even though they had twice followed him to home addresses in Dewsbury and Batley. In June 2004 further checks on his car registration did produce the name 'Sidique Khan'. Running this name through the database would have brought up details of his conversation with 'Bashful Dwarf', who was under investigation for supporting al-Qaida in Pakistan. At this point, they had their sights on a British extremist who was already known to have been close to the leader of the fertilizer-bomb plot and who had been associating with a man linked to al-Qaida. They knew all of this a year before the London bombings.

Six months after the fertilizer-bomb plotters were arrested, Sidique Khan filmed himself in a video farewell at his home in Leeds. Cradling his baby daughter in his arms, he kisses her on the head and speaks into the camera. 'Not got too long to go now and I'm going to really, really miss you. I absolutely love you to bits. You've been the happiest thing in my life. I'm doing what I'm doing for the sake of Islam.'

In November, Sidique Khan travelled to Pakistan once again, this time with Shehzad Tanweer. It remains unconfirmed but it is likely that the two men sought out their old al-Qaida contacts in the North-west Frontier Province. Judging by the finality of Sidique Khan's farewell message, he was not expecting to come back. It is possible that he intended to die fighting with the Taliban insurgents in Afghanistan. If so, his tactics abruptly changed.

On the morning of July 7, 2005 the nation awoke to news of simultaneous power cuts on the London Underground. The inevitable was swiftly confirmed: four coordinated terrorist attacks on the capital – three on the Tube, one on a bus – had taken place. Terrorists had murdered fifty-two people and injured 700 with crude but deadly home-made bombs.

Police forensic teams moved in, sifting through the twisted metal and torn flesh at the sites of the explosions. The first bomb had exploded on a Circle Line train in a tunnel between Liverpool Street and Aldgate stations; the second was detonated on another Circle Line train, just outside Edgware Road station; the third in a Piccadilly Line tunnel between King's Cross and Russell Square, with the fourth on a number 30 red double-decker bus in Tavistock Square.

Just before midnight on the day of the bombings, fragments of credit cards and membership cards in the names of Sidique Khan and Mr S. Tanweer were recovered at Aldgate. Evidence of a second card linked to a Sidique Khan was found at the scene of the Edgware Road attack the next day and shortly afterwards the police named Hasib Hussain and Germaine Lindsay as other prime suspects. Meanwhile MI5 technical experts were analysing fragments of a mobile phone SIM card found at the Edgware Road bomb site. When they ran the number through the MI5 database, it immediately registered a 'hit' on the 'Sidique Khan' they had on their files – the man at the Iqra bookshop in Leeds, whom they had recorded talking with 'Bashful Dwarf' from Luton in 2003. Other checks revealed that this was the same man they had photographed

and recorded in February and March 2004 when he was with Omar Khyam, the leader of the fertilizer-bomb plotters. They had been tracking the future leader of the London bombers, but had allowed him to slip through the net. According to an MI5 source, this failure cast 'a huge cloud' over the organization.

Within days of the bombings the focus of the investigation shifted to Leeds. The flat where the bombers had prepared their devices was quickly discovered. Abandoned equipment lay scattered around; a gas mask left by the sink had been used when boiling down hydrogen peroxide solution to make the explosives; plastic containers used to store the bombs were found in a bath filled with cold water, an attempt to keep the devices cool and stable. There was even a hand-written shopping list marked 'Things 2 Do'.

Here was direct evidence of pre-attack planning. It listed 'shrapnel' from B&Q; 'icepacks' and 'sun-blinds for the car' to keep the bombs cool during transport to London; fifteen kilograms of powdered masala spice, a vital ingredient for the home-made bombs, and, curiously, a reference to 'Chacha', which is the Urdu word for uncle. 'Chacha' was the code word used to refer to members of al-Qaida based in Kohát in Pakistan. On the basis of this connection I am convinced that, in the days before the July 7 attacks, Sidique Khan sought final approval from his al-Qaida leader in the Northwest Frontier Province.

On July 21, two weeks after the attacks, four other would-be suicide bombers struck in London: three on the Tube and one on a bus. This time, by good fortune, their devices failed to detonate and all four men were eventually caught and convicted. Only a flaw in the ratios of ingredients used to make the explosives saved London from another catastrophe. There are remarkable similarities between the two operations: both teams used triacetone triperoxide (TATP) explosives and both targeted the London Underground. It was no surprise to learn much later that Mukhtar Ibrahim, the leader of the July 21 bomb plot, had been out in Pakistan at the same time as Sidique Khan and Shehzad Tanweer. Like Khan, he had been under

surveillance a year before the attack, in August 2004. Like Khan, he was not considered to be a direct threat.

In the days after the July 7 attacks, I followed the police investigation as it moved north to Beeston, one of the poorest suburbs of Leeds. It had now been established that three of the four bombers had been living there. Viewed from the surrounding dales, Beeston resembles a rusting hulk, with its decks of red-brick terraced houses climbing and falling with the terrain, separated from the glass offices and chrome-plate bars of the affluent city centre by a hostile sweep of motorway. I walked past washing-hung alleys strewn with wheelie bins. Blue-and-white police tape fluttered in the breeze outside the houses where the suspected bombers had lived.

A woman I met on the street offered to talk to me, but only in the privacy of her home. She was afraid of reprisals, so on the condition of anonymity she explained how she had married into the extended family of one of the bombers. She had been shown propaganda videos in the Iqra centre, where Sidique Khan and Shehzad Tanweer used to meet. One local resident said that Khan had been a powerful figure who commanded respect for his work with drug addicts. Former colleagues at Hillside Primary School, where he had worked as a teaching assistant, told me how one of Britain's worst mass murderers had seemed a 'perfect role model' for the children.

Shehzad Tanweer's father, Mumtaz Tanweer, was a prominent Pakistani businessman in Beeston. He owned and ran South Leeds Fisheries, a fish and chip shop where his son worked after dropping out of university. The family were not giving any interviews, so I contacted one of Mumtaz Tanweer's business colleagues. 'Mr Mumtaz has been a friend of mine for thirty-five years,' I was told. 'His family are very hard-working, his son is number one. When we knew he was missing, we went to the mosque in Dewsbury, searching for him. Nobody had seen him. His father was terrified and said, "I've lost everything."'

'Which mosque in Dewsbury?' I asked.

'The Markaz: we went straight there.'

Retracing the route taken by Shehzad Tanweer's family on the night they discovered he was missing, I arrived in Dewsbury, a small town south of Leeds. The Dewsbury Markaz, as the mosque is known, is in a district named Savile Town, where the streets are overshadowed by the grime-blackened gritstone walls of textile mills. These mills once employed immigrants from the Indian subcontinent who arrived in England in their tens of thousands in the decades following the end of the Second World War. Dewsbury's wealth was founded on the heavy woollen trade and before this, on the production of shoddy, the name for poor-quality cloth produced by grinding down old rags. The mills are mostly silent now; the Asda supermarket employs more people than the largest remaining textile firm. But the workers who arrived from Pakistan and from Gujarat, the predominately Muslim province of north-west India, have stayed; more than eighty per cent of the population is Muslim. Four decades since they arrived in England they are even more isolated, both geographically and culturally, from the rest of the town.

The Dewsbury Markaz is the European headquarters of Tablighi Jamaat, a secretive organization based in Pakistan and New Delhi. While the organization strongly denies involvement with terrorist violence, it is of increasing interest to MI5. According to a British Home Office report, supporters in Pakistan helped to create the extremist group Harakat-ut-Jihad-ul-Islami, known as HUJI. The report states that HUJI 'has conducted kidnappings of foreigners, including Westerners (some Britons), some of whom were murdered.'

The British government's official account of the London bombings has now confirmed that Shehzad Tanweer spent time with Tablighi Jamaat at its Dewsbury headquarters in the months before the attack. Mohammed Sidique Khan is believed to have joined him there. The organization's supporters have also been implicated in other planned or actual terrorist atrocities in Europe. In January, Spain's Guardia Civil police arrested fourteen Tablighi Jamaat

followers in Barcelona, eleven of whom have since been charged with plotting to bomb the city's transport system. Kafeel Ahmed, the man who crashed a burning Jeep into Glasgow airport's passenger terminal last summer, also had links with Tablighi Jamaat in the Indian city of Bangalore.

With a standing capacity of 3,000, the Dewsbury Markaz, built in 1982, is one of the largest mosques in Britain. There is an Islamic school next to the mosque, which accepts both boarders and day pupils. I watched as about thirty teenage boys gathered in the yard. Dressed in simple robes, carrying small, cloth shoulder bags, they resembled a medieval religious order. They were preparing to leave for the weekend, travelling out on their mission, or *jamaat*, to bring back wayward Muslims into the fold of fundamentalist Islam. The older boys stay at mosques around the country; sometimes they travel abroad. Proselytizing is the core of the Tablighi doctrine.

I have since found out that the insularity of the Islamic school run by the movement in Dewsbury had been criticized by school inspectors three months before I visited in July 2005. An Ofsted investigation concluded that the school was overly concerned with religious instruction at the expense of mainstream education and that it provided poor preparation for life in multicultural Britain. Every morning was devoted to Islamic studies and memorizing the Qur'an; insufficient time was given to non-religious subjects in the afternoon. Unsurprisingly, it failed its inspection because 'a considerable amount of teaching is unsatisfactory or poor in National Curriculum subjects'.

Walking through the streets of Savile Town beyond the school gates, it is quite possible to believe that Muslims there simply want to get on with their own lives, unaffected by and indifferent to wider society. Most of the area's Muslim population are, like the Taliban movement, Deobandis, who regard themselves as Islamic purists, remaining close to the original teachings and life of the Prophet Muhammed. Strict Deobandis encourage women to remain at home and prohibit the free mixing of the sexes. Marriages are arranged. Deobandism was founded in nineteenth-century India, in the city of

Deoband, partly as a political reaction against British rule. After partition in 1947, a network of Deobandi Islamic schools or madrasas was established in Pakistan and after this the movement spread to the West, with the Pakstani diaspora. There are now twenty-seven Deobandi schools in Britain and many mosques are under Deobandi control; the leading Deobandi seminary is in the Lancashire town of Bury.

In Britain, there are naturally Deobandis who are prepared to interact with mainstream society but, on the whole, most orthodox followers seek to separate themselves from non-Muslims. In Savile Town the sense of isolation is profound. Women walk the streets hidden under their black burqas, mesh screens covering their eyes. The visual message of separation is stark, and it is being repeated in towns and cities throughout England.

Britain has become a different country since the July 7 attacks. The head of the Commission for Racial Equality, Trevor Phillips, who is a black Briton of Guyanese origin, has warned that, because of the cultural isolation of Muslims in so many British towns, we may be 'sleepwalking our way to segregation'. In many places segregation has already arrived. If you travel to Dewsbury, Bradford, Burnley or Rochdale, or any number of other post-industrial towns in the north of England or the Midlands, you will see Muslim communities living apart from the rest of society. One Pakistani taxi driver I interviewed in Birmingham bitterly regretted that his son had to go to 'an all-Asian school', because thirty years before, when he was a boy, society had been far more mixed. Yet the connection between social isolation and violent extremism is of course far from straightforward. Mohammed Sidique Khan did not come from a fundamentalist community. He once refused to have an arranged marriage because he was in love with the woman who became his wife, Hasina. She was the daughter of Farida Patel, a respected – and culturally liberal – community worker from Dewsbury, south of Leeds, who has been honoured by the Queen. It seems that both

families disapproved of the relationship. When I visited the cul-de-sac of neatly kept bungalows in Dewsbury where Hasina once lived with her parents, a neighbour described how the future leader of the London bombers would wait in his car outside her father's house, like any other teenager.

So how did Sidique Khan become a man prepared to murder his fellow citizens in the name of Allah? There are no simple answers. There are what the Security Services call the 'push factors', those forces that make recruits vulnerable to radicalization, as well as 'pull factors' from terrorist leaders and radicalizers, both in Britain and abroad. The strongest push factor is the alienation felt by many British Muslims in the country of their birth, the crises of identity, separateness and rejection with which they grapple. Under the influence of propagandists, this unease can be manipulated into a world view in which Islam is perceived to be at war with the secular West and with the kafir, with the unbeliever. From there it is a short step to convincing new recruits that murdering 'the enemies of Islam' will be rewarded in the next life. In the words of the radical cleric Abu Hamza, who preached for so long at the Finsbury Park mosque, 'Killing a kafir who is fighting you is okay. Killing a *kufr* for any reason, you can say it, it is okay – even if there is no reason for it. If a *kufr* goes in a Muslim country, he is like a cow, anybody can take him. That is the Islamic law, it is allowed.'

For more than a decade, until the London bombings, Britain was supine in the face of such verbal attacks. Extremist preachers were free to radicalize and recruit the disaffected Muslim youth because it was believed that to admonish them would be equivalent to criticizing a faith, even when they were inciting hatred. The failure of the British government to take robust action served only to strengthen the extremists, who felt increasingly invincible in Britain, and weaken the moderate mainstream Muslims who were too often too slow to denounce the extremists among them.

For many years the wider Muslim community failed to reject unequivocally the extremism being preached in the name of Islam.

When I interviewed mosque leaders about the July 7 attacks most conceded that the bombers were 'criminals', but they also refused to accept that it was jihadi theology inspired by the Qur'an that had given the bombers the confidence to kill themselves and others. This state of denial is exacerbated by the refusal of many British Muslims to trust the police. And conspiracy theories abound: large numbers of people simply do not believe that Muslims are involved in terrorist plots; they prefer to see the various plots as being part of a wider global anti-Islamic conspiracy, usually involving the Jews.

MI5 continues to infiltrate the British jihadi network and the quality of intelligence appears to be improving. In 2007, forty-two people were convicted of terrorist offences relating to sixteen different operations. Terrorist plots which could have resulted in thousands of deaths have been thwarted. However, even now, groups of extremists who used to be members of al-Muhajiroun, which was disbanded by Omar Bakri Mohammed in October 2004, are organizing meetings across Britain, drawing in the next generation of recruits at clandestine gatherings and rallies. There are as many as 200 indigenous active terrorist cells being monitored by MI5, with 4,000 British Muslims considered to be a threat to national security.

Few within the security services doubt that there will be another muderous terrorist attack in Britain before too long. 'You've got to be lucky every time, we've only got to be lucky once,' say some Islamist extremists I have met, paraphrasing an old IRA slogan. Improving the odds for the police and MI5 crucially depends on persuading the wider Muslim community to come forward with intelligence about extremism. Yet in my experience many people with useful information simply do not trust the police to be discreet, believing extremists are already working as double agents on the inside, or that the police fail to offer sufficient protection to informers. Some police forces, particularly those outside the major urban centres, are unused to gathering intelligence from the Muslim community, as I found out after I interviewed a woman who had

wanted to come forward with information.

Ayesha had arrived from the Far East to marry a British Muslim. Her family had chosen the wrong man; her husband turned out to be a leading member of an extremist group. Over the course of a year Ayesha found out that her husband was discussing how to carry out attacks on Britain. She told me she was asked if she would be prepared to wear a suicide vest and to blow herself up. When I interviewed her we went to some lengths to protect her identity, meeting well away from her home and disguising her appearance. Because of the gravity of her allegations we were obliged to inform the police. I explained that her life would be in danger if her identity was revealed, yet in an extraordinary act of recklessness the police force arranged to interview her at her local Muslim community centre, where she was known. Once there, she was persecuted for speaking to the media rather than praised for her bravery in coming forward with important intelligence. Another source was lost on that afternoon, and Ayesha's life was put in danger.

But I was to find out soon afterwards that there is another, more significant reason why the flow of intelligence to the police and Security Service has been slow: even some of the most respected Muslim leaders refuse to believe that terrorist plots are real.

Recently I visited one of the most senior Muslim leaders in Britain, Dr Mohammed Naseem, chairman of the Birmingham Central Mosque. A practising medical doctor, he has a reputation as a moderate. He organized books of condolence for the victims of the Madrid bombings and for Ken Bigley, the British hostage murdered in Iraq. We arranged to meet at his surgery, not far from the mosque. He invited me to his consulting rooms where a full-sized model of a human skeleton watched over us from one corner of the room. Dr Naseem has been scientifically trained and I expected to be able to have a rational discussion with him about Islam and terrorism. Yet when I asked about the July 7 attacks, he explained that Muslims in Britain were being framed.

I asked him about the video of Mohammed Sidique Khan

recorded just before the London bombings and released by al-Qaida after his death, in which, wearing a red and white headdress (a keffiyeh) and occasionally thrusting a pen at the camera, the young jihadist spoke of his willingness to die for Islam in 'obedience to the one true God, Allah'.

'The 7/7 video?' Dr Naseem said. 'Many youngsters feel they need to find a new identity.'

He paused.

'I suspect that video is fake.' ■

A still from Mohammed Sidique Khan's suicide video

www.granta.com
Jason Cowley talks to Richard Watson

THE TRIUMPH OF MUSIC
THE RISE OF COMPOSERS, MUSICIANS AND THEIR ART
Tim Blanning

"Trenchant, wise and richly ironic, Tim Blanning's book travels spectacular distances between Plato and Elton John, Baroque liturgy and Robbie Williams, opera seria and internet downloads. With a masterly eye for detail he explains why music and audiences are interdependent and reveals the enduring potency of music as a sovereign art."
—Jonathan Keates, author of *The Siege of Venice*
Belknap Press / new in cloth

THE PECULIAR LIFE OF SUNDAYS
Stephen Miller

From Augustine to Caesarius, through the Reformation and the Puritan flight from England, down through the ages to contemporary debates about Sunday worship, Stephen Miller explores the fascinating history of the Sabbath.
new in cloth

SEVEN DEADLY SINS
A VERY PARTIAL LIST
Aviad Kleinberg
Translated by Susan Emanuel

"*The Seven Sins* is a fascinating, amusing and highly readable book that offers a rethinking of our sins and passions through an examination of the Christian deadly sins…to which Kleinberg adds an eighth, self-righteousness."—*Ynet*
Belknap Press / new in cloth

HARVARD
UNIVERSITY
PRESS
www.hup.harvard.edu

Inside the British Jihad

REUTERS/AL ARABIYA

Abu Qatada, whose full name is Omar Uthman Abu Omar, was born in Bethlehem in 1960 but he is a Jordanian national. He has been accused of being al-Qaida's spiritual leader in Europe. Videos of his lectures were found in the Hamburg flat of Mohammed Atta, leader of the September 11 attacks, and terrorists have found justifications for violence in his teachings. He arrived in Britain in 1993, travelling on a forged passport. Having been granted asylum, he used London as a base for his political work for Algeria's Armed Islamic Group (GIA). He soon became known for his sermons arguing that non-Muslims and mainstream Muslims were legitimate targets for attack. In 2001, after the September 11 attacks, he went on the run to evade new anti-terrorism laws, which would have allowed his detention without trial. Following the London bombings in July 2005, the government started legal proceedings to deport him to Jordan, where he faces terrorism charges. At that time a British judge described him as 'a truly dangerous individual'. However, he has recently won an Appeal Court hearing against deportation and was released from custody in May. He now wears an electronic tag and is confined to his west London home for twenty-two hours a day. Much of the evidence against him comes from intelligence sources and intercepts. He has not been convicted in a British court and denies being linked to al-Qaida.

HUSSEIN MALLA/PA PHOTOS

Omar Bakri Mohammed, the self-styled 'Sheikh', was born in Syria in 1958. He is responsible for recruiting most of the extremists at the heart of the British jihad. After being expelled from Syria in 1977 for his membership of the Muslim Brotherhood, he studied in Cairo before setting up a cell of Hizb ut-Tahrir followers in Saudi Arabia. In 1983 he founded a new group in the Kingdom

called al-Muhajiroun but was expelled in 1986, after which he arrived in Britain seeking asylum. Given indefinite leave to remain, he became the leader of Hizb ut-Tahrir in Britain, inspiring young British Muslims with the dream of re-establishing the Islamic state or caliphate. After breaking with Hizb ut-Tahrir in 1996, Bakri Mohammed re-formed al-Muhajiroun, which targeted alienated and angry British Muslims in towns and cities across the country. After the September 11 attacks, he praised the hijackers as the 'magnificent nineteen'. Many leading British jihadists were members of al-Muhajiroun. The leader of the fertilizer-bomb plotters, Omar Khyam, was recruited in Crawley; one of Britain's first suicide bombers, Asif Hanif, who blew himself up in a bar in Tel Aviv, was another recruit, as were Abdullah Izzadeen and Sulayman Keeler, both of whom were recently convicted of terrorism offences. Bakri Mohammed set up overseas branches of the group in the United States and Pakistan, where local leaders developed links with al-Qaida. When he left Britain for a holiday in Lebanon in 2005 the Home Secretary banned him from returning.

REUTERS/WAEL LADKI

Abu Hamza, perhaps the best-known radical cleric in Britain, was born Mustafa Kamel Mustafa in Egypt in 1958. He arrived in Britain in 1979 and, after marrying a British woman, became a British citizen in 1981. After working as a nightclub bouncer, he became interested in Islamist politics and was inspired by the US-backed mujahedin forces in Afghanistan, who were fighting the Soviet occupation. In 1987 he is reported to have met Sheikh Abdullah Azzam, the spiritual leader of the Afghan mujahedin, an experience which motivated him to travel to Afghanistan for jihad. There he lost a hand and an eye, either in explosives training or mine clearance work. He returned to Britain in the early 1990s but quickly joined the new

front for jihad in Bosnia in 1993. Hamza is currently fighting extradition from Britain to the United States, where he has been indicted for setting up a terrorist training camp at Bly, Oregon, and for taking part in a conspiracy to kidnap twelve Western tourists in the Yemen in 1998.

Omar Sheikh was born in London in 1973 and was a student at the London School of Economics. In February 2002 a court in Pakistan sentenced him to death for the kidnapping and murder of Daniel Pearl, the *Wall Street Journal* reporter beheaded in Karachi in January 2002. The Pakistani government has stayed Omar Sheikh's execution while his links with the Pakistani intelligence service, the ISI, are investigated.

Sulayman (Simon) Keeler, a white English convert to Islam, was recruited by al-Muhajiroun in Crawley, where he grew up. In 2005 Keeler founded Ahl ul-Sunnah Wa al-Jamma, an Islamist group created as a successor to al-Muhajiroun. This year he was sentenced to four and a half years in prison for inciting terrorism and for terrorist fund-raising.

Izzadeen Abdullah (Trevor Brooks; Abu Izzadeen) was born in Hackney in 1976 and converted to Islam in 1994, when he was seventeen, and soon joined Omar Bakri Mohammed's al-Muhajiroun. He subsequently founded the Islamist group Al Ghurabaa. Convicted, with Sulayman Keeler, for terrorist offences, he is currently serving a four-and-a-half-year jail sentence.

Omar Khyam was born in 1981. He was the ringleader of the fertilizer-bomb plot to blow up the Bluewater shopping centre in Kent, exposed in 2004 by Operation Crevice. He was convicted for his part in the plot in 2007 and sentenced to life imprisonment along with four other defendants. He has since been convicted of

grievous bodily harm, after pouring boiling cooking oil over a fellow inmate at Frankland Prison in County Durham.

Anthony Garcia was born Abdulrahman Benouis in Algeria in 1982 but changed his name in order to pursue a career as a model. He was convicted in 2007 for his part in the fertilizer-bomb plot. He is currently serving a life sentence.

Salahuddin Amin was born in London in 1975 but was educated in Pakistan from the age of four, only returning to Britain twelve years later. Convicted for his part in the fertilizer-bomb plot, he claims to have been tortured and forced to give false testimony by the authorities in Pakistan, where he gave himself up in 2004.

Jawad Akbar, now serving a life sentence for his role in the fertilizer-bomb plot, was born in Pakistan in 1983 and moved to Crawley in 1992 at the age of eight. He attended Hazlewick School, where Omar Khyam was also a pupil. The jury at his trial was played a tape recording in which Akbar can be heard suggesting a bomb attack on the Ministry of Sound nightclub in London.

Waheed Mahmood was born in 1972 and lived in Crawley. The jury at the trial of the fertilizer-bomb plotters, which convicted him for his part, heard evidence that Mahmood had wanted to sell poisoned food and drink at football stadiums and attack gas and electricity networks. He had been employed by British Gas during the 1990s and had been working for Morrison Utility Services on a project for National Grid Transco at the time of the plot.

Abu Uzair was born Sajid Sharif in 1968 and trained as a civil engineer. In 2005 he became a founding member, with Sulayman Keeler, of Ahl ul-Sunnah Wa al-Jamma. Today he is free and continues to support jihadi ideology.

Hassan Butt was born in Luton in 1980. Following his expulsion from Wolverhampton University for Islamist activity, he became a spokesman for al-Muhajiroun. He has claimed to have helped as many as 600 British Muslims travel to Pakistan and Afghanistan for jihad. Since the London bombings on July 7, Butt has publicly renounced extremism and following the attack on Glasgow Airport in summer 2007 he met a minister from the Home Office who offered him financial support for his work to deradicalize young British Muslims. In May 2008 he was arrested under the Terrorism Act and held for twelve days by Greater Manchester Police before being released without charge.

On Tour in 2008

ENGLISH
NATIONAL
BALLET

The Sleeping Beauty
Reawaken the magic of the world's favourite fairy-tale
5 October - 14 December
Oxford New Theatre
Southampton Mayflower
Liverpool Empire
London Coliseum

Manon
Innocence corrupted by decadence
in a passionate French tragedy
22 October - 11 January
Bristol Hippodrome
Southampton Mayflower
Manchester Palace
London Coliseum

The Nutcracker
A magical Christmas treat for all the family
7 - 30 December
London Coliseum

Angelina's
Star Performance
The Little Star with Big Dreams stages
her first real live ballet
September - 20 November
National Tour

www.ballet.org.uk

National Tour Sponsor 2008

skyARTS

ARTS COUNCIL ENGLAND

Photo by Annabel Moeller. Charity no 140

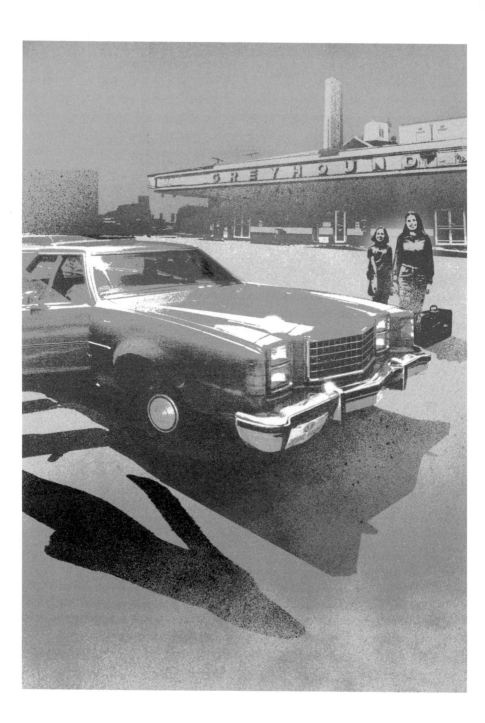

BROKEN STAR

Jennifer Haigh

ILLUSTRATION BY SHONAGH RAE

I met my aunt Melanie in the summer of 1974, an August of high bright days, so dry that my father had to oil our front lane to keep the dust down. I was fifteen, midway through high school and deadened by its sameness. I could scarcely remember what had preceded it, or begin to imagine what might follow.

'You don't remember me, do you? You were so little when I left.' Melanie climbed into the front seat of our station wagon, next to my father. This was my mother's usual place, surrendered out of courtesy since Melanie was a guest. She had arrived with her stepdaughter Tilly on the Greyhound bus from Pensacola, Florida. Tilly, who was eight, shared the back seat with me and my mother.

'Not exactly,' I said, though I had heard about Melanie my whole life: my mother's sister, the youngest of seven, the midlife baby who'd surprised my grandmother after two miscarriages. *I was an 'oops'*, Melanie would tell me later, a confession that shocked and thrilled me. I'd never heard an adult allude to such matters. We were not that kind of family.

There was a rustling sound as she rifled through her shopping bags. 'For Regina,' she said, handing me a small unwrapped box. Inside was a pair of earrings, the dangling kind I admired, decorated with tiny seashells. These were made for pierced ears, so I wouldn't be able to wear them.

'They're beautiful,' I said. 'Thank you.'

My mother glanced at the earrings. She didn't care about jewellery, but feigned interest to be polite. 'Very nice,' she said. 'But Melanie, you shouldn't have.'

She greeted all presents this way – *you shouldn't have* – no matter how worthy the occasion or how trifling the gift. It was a habit born of embarrassment. No gift – even one she'd always wished for – was worth drawing attention to herself.

Melanie seemed not to have this problem. On the ride home she talked non-stop: the difference in weather from Florida to Pennsylvania, the assortment of characters she and Tilly had met along the way. She imitated the bayou accent of the bus driver, so thick that the names of cities they'd stopped in – Savannah, Georgia; Raleigh, North Carolina – were completely unintelligible. My father chuckled appreciatively. My mother giggled like a schoolgirl, covering her mouth with her hand.

Melanie had been gone for twelve years, the only one of my relatives who lived away. 'Away', in my family, meant anywhere outside central Pennsylvania, the quiet stretch of country, bordered by highways and Amish, where we'd farmed for four generations. Philadelphia was away. Pittsburgh, a grimy city of immigrants and steel mills, was, emphatically, away.

Melanie had left after graduating from high school. She attended secretarial school in Washington, DC, and worked as a typist at the Department of the Interior before marrying Uncle Dan and moving to a naval base down south. I knew her face only from photographs, the half-dozen that decorated my grandmother's parlour. One in particular impressed me, her high school graduation portrait:

Melanie in an off-the-shoulder blouse of glamorous black, a colour nobody much wore in those days, certainly not young girls. 'It's a drape,' my mother explained. 'They made all the girls wear it. Don't ask me why.' She said it in the impatient tone I recognized, the one that meant I was interested in the wrong things.

I never mentioned the drape again, but I thought about it a great deal, Melanie being draped by someone, a photographer presumably. It seemed a reverent gesture, exquisitely romantic. In the photo Melanie's dark hair was spread across her shoulders, her chin tipped at the unnatural angle favoured by school photographers. The whole presentation was rather theatrical, and Melanie smiled as though she knew this but was simply playing along. Her attitude, though I didn't yet know the word for it, was ironic, and it was this quality that delighted me.

Now, in person, Melanie looked much the same as she had in the photo, though she had just turned thirty, an age I did not consider young. By thirty my female cousins were stout matrons: large bosoms firmly corseted, hair cut and permed into helmets of tight curls. Melanie's hair hung nearly to her waist, and she wore the kind of wide-bottomed blue jeans I saw in magazines but didn't own; they were impractical for farm chores. She looked the way girls my age were supposed to look, while I – in my sleeveless blouse and home-made skirt, the flowered pattern not quite matching at the seams – looked like a younger version of my mother.

Night was falling as we left the bus station, an amenity which, until then, I hadn't known the town possessed. I went to high school in town – this involved a half-hour ride on a rickety school bus – but apart from the main streets, I'd spent little time there. The bus station was located on a dark side street behind a tyre factory. My father had escorted us at my mother's insistence, though he grumbled that this was unnecessary. The neighbourhood was perfectly safe.

I was beginning to notice how often they had such conversations: my mother asking for protection, my father reluctant to provide it. At home she was a model of efficiency, a take-charge housekeeper

who structured my free time around endless daily chores; but in the outside world she was rather timid. My father had taught her to drive early in their marriage, but she refused to go any further than the grocery store. She drove slowly, nervously, and only on the back roads. The Pennsylvania Turnpike, with its three lanes in each direction, scared her witless.

Back at the house, my father carried Melanie's suitcase upstairs to the sewing room, whose couch opened into a bed. Tilly would sleep in my room. 'Give your cousin the bottom bunk,' I was instructed, though Tilly wasn't really my cousin, being Uncle Dan's from a previous marriage. This was how my mother said it: 'from a previous marriage', as though there'd been more than one.

I helped Tilly unpack her shorts and T-shirts. She was a skinny little thing, red-haired, with a sharp chin and a dark band of freckles across the bridge of her nose, so that from a distance she seemed to be wearing a Band-Aid.

'Why do you have bunk beds?' she asked.

'For sleepovers,' I said, though technically this had never happened. In the third grade, I'd been allowed to invite Donna Holtz to spend the night. Homesick, she had cried all evening, until my father drove her the twenty miles back to town. After that, no more sleepovers.

Tilly considered. 'Maybe,' she said judiciously. 'Or maybe they wanted to have more kids.'

'Nah,' I said, as though the idea had been discussed and dismissed. In fact, the possibility had never occurred to me.

'Anyway, it doesn't matter,' she said, climbing into bed. 'They're too old now.'

I turned off the light and in a few minutes I heard Tilly snoring in the bunk below. I lay awake a long time thinking about what she had said. I couldn't imagine my mother pregnant, let alone doing what was necessary to get that way. Like any farm girl, I understood the mechanics of reproduction. I had once snuck into my uncle Wilmer's barn while Lassie, a beautiful little mare, was being bred, a polite term that doesn't convey the brutality of the operation. I was

squeamish about applying that model to any human couple, let alone my parents. At that age I was more interested in the runway leading up to such intimacies, the kissing and ardent glances, none of which I had experienced myself.

Drifting off to sleep, I found myself thinking of Melanie and Uncle Dan, who had met on the beach at Ocean City, Maryland. I'd been to the shore only once, on a rare family vacation, but I still dreamed of it. Not the ocean itself, but the human tableau running alongside it; the hundreds of strange, bare bodies on display, decorated with bright bathing suits. It was easy to place Melanie on that beach. I'd never seen Uncle Dan, not even a picture; but I imagined him tall and dark, with a hairy chest like Burt Reynolds.

I was nearly asleep when I heard Tilly sniffling.

'What's the matter?' I whispered. 'Did you have a bad dream?'

'I miss my dad,' she wailed.

This surprised me, because Tilly seemed older than her years. In fact she was the same age Donna Holtz had been at the time of our sleepover, and much farther from home.

'It's just temporary. You'll see him soon enough.'

'No, I won't.' Tilly inhaled wetly. 'We're never going back.'

'Don't be silly,' I said, because that's what my mother would've said.

For a long time Tilly didn't speak.

'Why would you think that?' I whispered. 'Did Melanie say that?'

'No,' Tilly said. 'I just know.'

I kept quiet about what Tilly had said. It was easy to do, since I rarely saw my parents during the day. August is busy on a farm and we were each occupied with separate chores. I would see my mother at suppertime and my father not even then; most nights he had meetings at the Grange Hall, to prepare for the county fair. That year he was a judge in two categories, Swine and Youth Dairy Cattle. He felt out of his depth with the swine – we hadn't raised piglets in years – but with the calves he was more than confident. I'd heard it said my whole life,

by neighbours and uncles and men from church, their grave inflection giving it the weight of a proverb: *Albert Yahner knows cattle.*

The fair had been a fixture of my childhood, as thrilling as Christmas, as anticipated and beloved. For six days each September there would be crowd and commotion, the Ferris wheel, the sweet greasy aroma of frying potatoes and funnel cakes. As a little girl I'd walked the midway flanked by my parents. Holding their hands, I kept up a steady chatter, enjoying their nearness, their protection from the unaccustomed crowd. When I got older, I entered animals in the youth competitions. I showed rabbits three years in a row and at twelve, a Jersey calf named Buttercup, who took second place in her class.

Three years later, my father still pestered me to raise another calf. 'Someday,' I told him. The truth was, I had no intention of doing this; given the choice, I would skip the fair altogether. I was embarrassed, now, by the cowboy music, the livestock smell, the farm boys in their stiff new dungarees, hair slicked back as if for church. Last year I'd stayed close to the booth where I sold raffle tickets to raise money for the 4-H club, keeping a nervous lookout for my schoolmates, the town girls in their sundresses and pretty sandals. How I coveted those sandals! I loved them precisely because they were so impractical, bound to get ruined in the gravel and muck. The girls came in groups of three or four, whispering and sometimes breaking out in loud laughter. They might have been laughing at anything, but I felt with a deep certainty that they were mocking people like my parents. My mother in her housedress and dark lipstick, flushed with excitement, clinging to my father's arm.

'It's about that time, isn't it?' Melanie asked at supper. 'The fair. God, I used to love the fair.'

'It's a lot of aggravation, if you ask me,' my mother said, passing a platter of fried chicken. 'Bert will be relieved when it's over.'

'I think he likes it,' I said.

'It's too much for him. Since his heart attack.'

'What about you, Gina?' Melanie had taken to shortening my name, which delighted me. I'd never had a nickname before.

'I probably won't go,' I said, avoiding my mother's eyes. 'I'll have homework then. It's the first week of school.'

'You've got to be kidding.' Melanie took the platter. 'Won't all your friends be there?'

My mother stared at me in bewilderment. 'I don't know what's come over you.'

'Don't listen to her, Peg.' Melanie heaped her plate with potato salad. For a small person she had a huge appetite. 'She's going to the fair.'

Melanie was a late riser. It was ten, ten-thirty by the time she wandered into the kitchen in her nightgown. Even Tilly slept until nine. My mother tolerated this for two days. The third morning she enlisted them to work in the kitchen, putting up bread-and-butter pickles. She and Tilly picked the cucumbers, brought them in from the garden and scrubbed them at the sink. Melanie had the best job, slicing them into thin rounds, and I had the worst, sterilizing the Ball jars. Using metal tongs, I placed them four at a time in a huge cauldron of boiling water, a steamy, miserable operation that kept me in front of the blazing stove in the August heat.

'Your mother runs a tight ship, Gina.' Melanie sat perched on a high stool in front of a breezy window. 'Jesus, you'll be glad to go back to school.'

'Ten more days,' I said, grinning. I'd forgotten – it was easy to forget – that Melanie had been a farm kid too.

'Do they still make you write that essay, "What I Did on Summer Vacation"?'

'Some vacation,' I said, mopping my forehead with a towel.

'My vacation was just super,' Melanie said in a simpering voice. 'I watered two hundred head of dairy cattle.'

'I hauled manure a quarter-mile to the garden,' I added.

'I sat by the highway all day in the blazing sun,' said Melanie, 'and I sold six ears of corn.'

I laughed so hard no sound came out, a feeling both delicious and

frightening. Through the open window I saw my mother come up the garden path with another bushel of cucumbers.

'I put up a million quarts of bread-and-butter pickles,' Melanie continued. 'For God's sake! Does anybody *like* bread-and-butter pickles?' Then she noticed the expression on my face. 'Gina? What's the matter?'

My mother stood in the doorway, her cheeks flaming. The screen door spanked shut behind her. She glanced around the kitchen: the steam rising from the stove, the counters, covered with old towels, where I'd set the jars to dry.

'You don't have to help if you don't want to,' she said, an odd tremor in her voice.

'Peg,' said Melanie, turning to face her. 'We were just having fun.'

My mother set her basket on the table. 'Don't bother with these. I guess we have enough.'

'How long is Melanie going to stay?' I asked my mother.

We were preparing Sunday dinner – roast beef, potatoes and carrots, a relish plate of pickled beets and my mother's vinegar cabbage, what we called 'chow-chow'. This was the standard menu for when the relatives came to dinner. For summer visits like this one, a platter of cut vegetables was added, whatever was ripening in the garden; but otherwise my mother made no concession to the season. Even today, maybe the hottest of the year, she didn't consider a barbecue or cold supper, to avoid firing the oven all afternoon.

'You never know with Melanie. You can't pin her down.' She opened the oven door. A wave of heat smacked my bare legs.

'But doesn't Tilly have school?' My own classes would begin in a week, an event I looked forward to with a mix of excitement and dread.

'Not for another month. The Florida schools start later. The heat, I suppose.'

The screen door slammed and my father appeared, still dressed in his church clothes. His sleeves were rolled above his elbows. Sweat

rings showed under the arms of his white shirt.

'Makes sense, if you ask me.' He turned on the faucet and scrubbed his hands and forearms, streaked with farm dirt. My mother frowned but said nothing, just watched the filthy water pool in the sink.

I persisted. 'A month, then?'

'Goodness, no. I'm sure Dan will want her back before then. A week at the most.'

My father raised his eyebrows. 'A week is a long time.'

'Don't be silly. She's my baby sister. Who knows when we'll see her again?' My mother arranged tomato slices on a plate. 'It won't kill Regina to share her room for a week. When I was a girl we slept three to a bed, except for George.'

This was not new information. I'd heard my whole life that I'd been spoiled by having my own room. (My uncle George, the one boy in his family, had been similarly pampered, a privilege he'd apparently paid for by being killed in the war, long before I was born.) I was often treated to sermons on the value of sharing, wearing hand-me-downs and waiting in line for the bathroom – lessons I, the first only-child on either the Yahner or the Schultheis side of my family, had failed to learn. I didn't have the nerve to protest that I hadn't *chosen* to be an only child, that my parents, who'd married late, were to blame. An eldest son, my father had spent his twenties and thirties running the Yahner farm, supporting his younger siblings and widowed mother. Even if he'd wanted to marry, my mother often said, where would he have found the time? Her own reasons for waiting were less clear, and more delicate. Plain and awkward, she had always been a homebody. Because of her shyness, school had been torture; when she dropped out of eleventh grade, her sisters were amazed that she'd lasted so long. My aunts agreed on this point: Peg was lucky to have found a husband, even one twenty years older. This was repeated throughout my childhood, so often that it never struck me as cruel. *Peg is lucky to have a husband at all.*

My aunts – Rosemary, Velva and Fern – were brisk, no-nonsense women who'd married in their teens and raised large families. Their children were grown now, with babies of their own. These

grandchildren were the subject of much discussion. *Two-and-a-half, and still in diapers. JoAnn lets him sleep in bed with her and Doug. I can't see why he puts up with it.* Occasionally, one of the aunts would notice that I was listening, as I stirred the gravy or fetched bottles of root beer for the men. *Remember this when you have babies, Regina. Before you know it, you'll be toilet-training your own.* These comments thrilled and perplexed me. To my knowledge, no boy had ever looked at me twice. What made my aunts so certain that, *before I knew it,* one would want to marry me? Explain this, I wanted to say. Explain how it happens.

It seemed to me then, and still does, that my aunts were made by marriage, that every defining feature of their lives – the children and grandchildren, the canning and cooking and crafting skills each possessed – was intimately connected to that long-ago moment of being chosen. My uncles Wilmer, Dick and Bill were like all the men I knew, soybean and dairy farmers who spoke rarely and then mainly about the weather. Yet unlikely as it seemed, I accepted that these men had the power to transform. My aunts had been pretty, lively girls – one stubborn, one mischievous, one coquettish, according to my mother. Yet somehow all three had matured into exactly the same woman: plump, cheerful, adept at pie-making and counted cross-stitch, smelling of vanilla and Rose Milk hand lotion. That I would someday become that same woman terrified me. My only greater fear was that nobody would choose me and I would become nothing.

The aunts and uncles arrived promptly at two, a strange time to eat a large meal – too late for lunch, too early for supper – but this was a Schultheis Sunday tradition. After spending all morning in church, the hostess needed a few hours to get the cooking underway.

'Hi stranger,' said Aunt Velva, giving Melanie a squeeze. 'Didn't you look pretty this morning? I just love that white dress.'

'Thank you.' Melanie winked at me over Velva's shoulder. She had borrowed the dress from my closet, after coming to the breakfast table in a printed sundress that tied behind her neck like a halter top, leaving her back and shoulders bare.

'Melanie, you can't,' my mother had said when Melanie came down the stairs.

Melanie shrugged. 'It's this or blue jeans. It's the only dress I brought.'

'Wear something of mine,' my mother suggested, though nothing in her closet was likely to fit. She wasn't fat, but tall and large-boned, with broad hips and shoulders. 'Or Regina's.'

'I don't mind,' I said. 'You're welcome to wear anything you like.'

Melanie followed me upstairs. 'I forgot all about church,' she said with a conspiratorial laugh, as though this were a private joke between us. 'Honestly, I haven't been in years.'

I stared at her in wonderment. It's hard to credit, now, how exotic I found this. It was as if I'd just discovered that Melanie could fly.

'Really? Never?'

'Nope. And God hasn't struck me dead.' She threw open my closet door and rifled through the dresses and blouses, stopping to admire a skirt I'd made that summer. 'This is pretty, but I don't think it will fit.'

'You're skinnier than I am,' I said, though that didn't describe it. Melanie had small breasts, a narrow waist, sharply curving hips. My body had the same features, or was beginning to; but these were recent developments. I wasn't used to seeing myself that way.

She gave me a playful shove. 'No, silly. We're the same size. You wear your clothes too big.'

I blinked. My mother bought patterns in size fourteen when she could have worn a twelve. I'd never realized I did the same thing.

Melanie chose a simple white dress I'd never liked, feeling exposed by its plainness. I turned my back politely as she untied her sundress. 'You'll need a slip with that,' I told her, digging through a bureau drawer. I couldn't bring myself to say, *You'll need a bra.*

Now she had changed back into blue jeans, though the rest of us were still in Sunday clothes. Even Tilly wore the dressiest outfit Melanie had packed for her, a denim skirt and blouse.

'And who is this little princess?' Aunt Fern asked, patting Tilly's

head. 'Honey, we're so happy to have you here. We've been hearing about you for ages.'

This was a blatant untruth. Though Melanie's name came up often in family conversations, no one ever spoke of Uncle Dan, let alone his daughter.

Tilly blossomed under the aunts' attention, guzzling cream soda and eating Velva's lemon drop cookies. Watching her, I felt lonely for my childhood, when the aunts had been at the centre of my small universe. I had especially adored Elsie, the oldest aunt, who until she died of kidney failure had spoiled me with small presents – knitting needles, beautiful buttons – prompting protests (*You shouldn't have*) from my mother. Recently, though, the aunts had become less interesting to me, their company less dear. They had always fussed over me, the youngest of the girl cousins; but it was no longer the type of attention I craved. I wanted them to notice the ways I differed from JoAnn and Prudence and Theresa and Ruth: my love of reading, my high marks in school. Of course, those differences weren't visible and I was too shy to speak of them. But at the time, that didn't occur to me.

The fair opened on a Monday, with a horse show and equipment expo, nothing I cared about. Tuesday would be barn games and harness racing; Wednesday, the milking contest and tractor pull. This year I begged off, complaining – in whispered tones, to my mother – of menstrual cramps. 'I'll be better by the weekend,' I told her. The most popular events would be held then – the Beef Cattle judging, the aerial show. Saturday night was the grand finale, an outdoor dance with a live band on the stage behind the Ag Hall.

We drove there in the pickup, my father, Melanie and I. My mother had gone ahead of us, taking Tilly with her, to sell baked goods at the Church of the Brethren tent. My father left us at the main gate and we wandered into the Ag Hall, past booths showing pies and needlecrafts, macramé and ceramics, hooked rugs and intricately pieced quilts.

'Wait. Look at that,' Melanie said.

The winning quilt hung against a makeshift wall, a blue ribbon pinned to its corner. The pattern was classic, an eight-pointed star on a white background, surrounded by a jagged border. It was the border that was most difficult to execute: sixteen sharp points, folding out from the original star like a paper snowflake. The design was pieced with snippets of blue fabric – ginghams and plaids and paisleys and sprigged muslins, all in shades of blue.

'It's beautiful,' Melanie said. She ran her hands over the quilt, admiring the delicate stitching. Only then did I notice the name on the entry tag.

'That's Mom's. It's an old pattern. Broken Star.' I stared at the quilt, ashamed I hadn't recognized it. For most of the summer, my mother had spent evenings alone in her sewing room. She'd been working on the quilt for months and I had never bothered to take a look.

'Peggy's amazing,' Melanie said softly. 'She can do anything.'

This stunned me. I had never thought of my mother that way.

Over Melanie's shoulder I saw a group of boys trotting through the expo hall. 'Pretend like we're talking,' I told her.

'We are talking.' She lowered her voice to a whisper. 'Why? Did you see somebody you know?'

'Those boys are in my class. Don't look.'

'I won't.' She leaned towards me as if whispering something in my ear. Then she laughed loud and bright, a perfect imitation of the town girls in my class.

The boys approached us. 'What's so funny?' said the tall one, Darren Wolf. For two years he'd sat in front of me in homeroom, the luck of alphabetical order. I knew all his shirts, how the rear seam followed the shape of his shoulders, how his blond hair curled over the collars. I couldn't recall him ever looking at me, or saying a word.

'None of your business,' Melanie said tartly. 'Gina, don't tell them.'

'Hi Regina,' said the other boy, Philip Schrey. We were in the same geometry class, but I was surprised that he knew my name.

'Regina,' said Darren Wolf. 'Is this your sister?'

'Kind of,' Melanie said, giggling.

'Do you go to Central?'

'Did,' she said. 'I graduated.'

Darren Wolf nodded as though he'd suspected as much. 'You girls going over to the dance?' he asked, though he was clearly asking Melanie.

Yes, I thought. *Just say yes.*

'In a minute,' she said. 'We're waiting for some people. We'll see you over there.'

'Okay then,' said Darren Wolf.

'See you,' said Philip Schrey.

When they were safely away, Melanie grabbed my hand. 'Do you go to Central?' she asked in a gruff voice.

We both shrieked with laughter.

August cooled into September. A dusting of yellow appeared on the trees. Each morning I trudged down the lane to wait for the school bus. Still Melanie didn't leave.

One morning I woke to find Tilly's bunk empty. Downstairs I found my mother at the stove, frying bacon and eggs. Fresh coffee bubbled in the percolator.

'Where's Tilly?' I asked.

'She's spending the day with Fern. Melanie, breakfast!' she called, scraping eggs on to a plate.

I heard loud footsteps above, the clatter of Melanie's wooden sandals on the stairs.

'Good morning!' she said breathlessly, giving my shoulder a squeeze. To my astonishment she was fully dressed, a poncho slung over her arm. She sat at the table and tucked into her breakfast.

'Regina, drink your milk,' my mother said. I noticed, then, her high colour, her cheeks flushed with agitation or excitement.

'What's going on?' I asked.

'We're going to Philadelphia,' Melanie said.

'You and mom?' To my knowledge, my mother had never been to Philadelphia in her life.

'Yep.'

In my half-asleep state I watched Melanie eat, stung by the unfairness of it all. Once, as a little girl, I'd been allowed to stay up until midnight on New Year's Eve, to watch the celebration on television; but I fell asleep before eleven. I awoke hours later in my own bed, where my father had carried me. I lay awake until sunrise, fuming at the injustice, heartbroken that I had missed my chance.

'Can I come?'

'Regina, don't be silly,' said my mother. 'It's a school day.'

'I don't care.' I felt suddenly alert, shocked awake by my own bravery. 'We never go anywhere.'

She stared at me in astonishment. I held my breath, because there was more I could have said: *Because you're afraid of everything. I'm stuck here because of you.*

Melanie took her plate to the sink. 'Peg, let her come. She can go to school any time. There are more important things.'

My mother started to speak, but Melanie interrupted her. 'Please, Peggy? I want her to come.'

Then a remarkable thing happened. My mother relented. I couldn't imagine why. I would wonder, later, about her reasons; but at the time I was too excited to care. Maybe I thought that with her fear of crowds and strangers, she felt safer with an extra body along. We set out in the station wagon, driving east into the blinding sun. The air had turned cold overnight, but the ground was still warm. Steam rose from the Yoders' bean fields on either side of the road, a ghostly haze that parted to let us pass. Melanie drove, with a speed and joyful carelessness that exhilarated me: the windows open, her long hair billowing in the breeze, Carole King on the radio, an AM station crackling with static. My mother sat beside her, clutching the door handle. If my father had been driving, she would have scolded him: *Bert, slow down. You'll get us killed.* But to Melanie she didn't say a word.

We approached Philadelphia just before noon, which surprised me. I'd imagined it much farther away. The city itself was a revelation – the tall skyline, the Schuylkill busy with boat traffic. We exited the highway and made a series of turns down busy boulevards. As we neared the city centre Melanie pulled over to look at a map.

'Let's stop here,' I suggested, staring out the window. Across the street was a small public park, crowded with people enjoying the midday sun.

'Sure,' said Melanie, cutting the engine.

'Melanie, really,' my mother said.

'There's an ice-cream stand.' Melanie pointed. 'I want an ice cream.'

We got out of the car and crossed the street, my mother hugging her purse to her chest.

'Three strawberry cones,' Melanie told the man at the window. She reached into the pocket of her jeans.

'Save your money,' my mother said, opening her purse.

I spotted an empty park bench and Melanie sat in the middle, her legs tucked up under her. I did the same.

'Sit like a lady,' my mother told me. 'Melanie, you're a bad influence.'

Melanie laughed. 'It's comfortable this way.'

We sat watching people pass: men in suits, smoking cigarettes; well-dressed women toting shopping bags; black maids in uniform pushing baby carriages. They were the sort of people I didn't see in everyday life. I could have sat there for hours.

'It's getting late,' my mother said.

Melanie licked her fingers. 'I could eat another one,' she said. 'Gina, could you eat another one?'

'Definitely,' I said.

'We could, you know.' She laid her head on my shoulder. 'We could eat ice cream all day long.'

'Melanie!' my mother said, so sharply that heads turned in our direction. Her anger startled me. I couldn't remember the last time I'd heard her raise her voice.

'Just kidding,' Melanie said, rising. 'Jesus, Peggy. It was a joke.'

We crossed the street and got into the car. Melanie drove down a narrow street and then another, barely wide enough for one car. The closeness frightened and delighted me: the houses and store fronts abutting, with no space between buildings, the pedestrians – a different crowd now, young and longhaired – crossing at random, mere feet from our car.

'Where are we going?' I asked for the first time.

Melanie didn't answer. Finally my mother spoke. 'Your aunt has an appointment.' Something in her tone, her way of referring to Melanie – *your aunt* – warned me. I didn't ask again.

'Look for number one-twenty,' Melanie said. 'It should be on the left.'

I was the first to spot the building, a narrow brick house with a dilapidated porch. Melanie parked and we went inside. We climbed a graceful old staircase to the second floor. The steps were covered in hexagonal tiles no bigger than quarters. The spaces between the tiles were filled in with grime.

At the end of the corridor we went into an office. A brass plate on the door read INTERNAL MEDICINE. We stepped into a dingy waiting room: mismatched chairs covered in green vinyl, outdated magazines – *McCall's*, the *Saturday Evening Post* – piled on a table in the corner.

I'm not sure how long we waited after Melanie's name was called. My mother paged through a *Ladies' Home Journal*, from front to back. Then she started over again, reading it back to front.

Outside the air had turned colder, the sky darkly clouded, as if the brilliant morning were something I'd dreamed. Slowly we crossed the street to the car, Melanie leaning heavily on my mother. I followed behind. They seemed to have forgotten I was there.

I watched as Melanie lowered herself into the driver's seat. When she turned the key in the ignition, the radio came on, a patter of muted trumpets. My mother reached to turn it off.

'No,' Melanie said. 'I like that song.'

She drove us out of the city and on to the Turnpike. No one spoke. Then, suddenly, she pulled over to the side of the road.

'I'm bleeding.' Her voice sounded strange, low down in her throat. 'I can feel it. Peggy, you'll have to drive.'

My mother stared at her wide-eyed. 'Melanie, I can't.'

'Why not?' Melanie turned to me, her eyes pleading. 'Gina?'

I shook my head mutely, shamed by my uselessness. I wouldn't be sixteen for two months. My father had promised to give me driving lessons, but so far I hadn't so much as turned the key in the ignition.

'Peggy, please.' Melanie got out of the car, her hand low on her belly, and opened the rear door. I climbed out and took the passenger seat up front. I will never forget the look on my mother's face as she took the wheel. She found the lever beneath the seat and slid herself forward, so that her face was inches from the windshield. Then she shifted into first gear and we rolled into the right lane. A shrieking sound as the car behind us slammed its brakes. My mother gasped.

'It's okay,' I said. 'Just give it some gas. You're doing fine.'

In the left lane cars whizzed past. My mother didn't answer. She kept a tight grip on the steering wheel, her eyes on the road.

'It'll be okay, Mom,' I said. 'Just keep driving.'

For a long time neither of us spoke. Once, twice, Melanie moaned softly from the back seat.

'Is she all right?' I asked.

My mother shifted into third, grinding the gears. An eighteen-wheeler screamed past us, its headlights blazing. She shielded her eyes.

'It's hard to look,' she said. 'Regina, I'm so scared. I just want to close my eyes.'

It was dark when we arrived back at the house. My father's truck was gone. Melanie went immediately to bed, my mother to the kitchen. She filled the percolator and took carrots from the refrigerator, a couple of pork chops.

'I'm not hungry,' she said suddenly. 'Are you hungry?'

'Not really,' I said.

When the coffee was ready she poured me a cup, something she had never done.

Across the kitchen table she explained how Melanie felt trapped with Uncle Dan, who had a terrible temper and sometimes hit her.

'Why?' Whether it was the news or the caffeine I can't say, but for the first time in my life I felt my heart.

'He's an animal.'

I was as shocked as if she'd spoken an obscenity. I'd never heard her say an unkind word about anybody.

'That's no way to raise a child,' she said haltingly. 'Can you imagine? Seeing his father behave that way.

'It's for the best,' she said softly, the last words I'd hear her say on the subject.

My father's truck pulled into the driveway then and my mother busied herself at the stove, laying the pork chops in a pan. I poured my coffee down the sink. The smell nauseated me. I have not drunk coffee since.

When I came home from school the following day, Melanie and Tilly were gone.

It was time, my mother explained. They'd been staying at our house for nearly a month.

A change came over her after Melanie left. For two days, three, her bedroom door was closed when I came home from school. 'She's feeling poorly,' my father said when I asked. 'A humdinger of a headache.' Baking and canning seemed more effort than she could muster. The last of the tomatoes rotted on the vine.

I could have lent a hand in the garden, but I didn't. I was preoccupied with my own concerns. Most nights I had long conversations with Philip Schrey, who'd asked for help with geometry homework and begun calling me on the phone. These phone calls – the waiting and planning, the delight when they

occurred and the crushing disappointment when they didn't – culminated in our first date, to see *The Towering Inferno* at the Regal Theatre in town. After that we ate lunch together in the school cafeteria. We went to football or basketball games on Friday nights. This new dimension of my life occupied me completely. My mother's difficulties didn't interest me at all.

We never spoke of the trip to Philadelphia. My mother didn't mention Melanie for months. A card arrived at Christmastime, with a Florida postmark. Inside was a single handwritten line: *Thanks for everything. Love, Melanie, Dan and Tilly.*

Years passed and I stopped thinking about that summer. Soon the slow August days were lost to me forever; it seemed, often, that I had no time to think. I went to college, worked, married a much older man and moved to a different country – feeling always that the world moved too fast for me, that I'd been raised to live at a gentler pace. In my late thirties I looked up and noticed that my parents were gone, the farm sold. Each year I considered sending a hundred Christmas cards, via airmail, to the dozens of Yahner and Schultheis relatives; but I never actually did this. My reasons were laziness and lingering guilt: I had neglected to invite my aunts to my wedding, a slight that, if they'd known about it, would have hurt them. I understood this, just as I understood that nothing – certainly not a secular City Hall wedding – could have induced Velva or Fern to travel to New York. Thinking of them made me sad and ashamed, so I stopped thinking of them. It wasn't hard to do. My interest in family had died with my mother. Without her I didn't see the point.

My first book was published the year we returned home from Sweden – a slender collection of short stories that seemed, and was, destined for the remainder bin. My publisher made a brief effort at promoting it, with a handful of signings at bookstores in the south and north-east. It was at one of these signings that I saw a familiar face, though I couldn't place it immediately. The woman was slight and red-haired, my age or a bit younger. 'Regina,' she said. 'Do you

remember me?'

I looked at her closely. Through the heavy make-up I could discern a dark band of freckles, crossing her nose like a bandage.

Tilly lived in Atlanta now, married to a linesman for Georgia Power. They had two daughters. She'd seen my photo in the Arts section of the newspaper and recognized me immediately, despite the unfamiliar last name. 'I'm so proud of you,' she said. 'Melanie would be so proud.'

Melanie. After all these years it affected me strangely, like the name of my first love. 'How is she?' I asked. 'Are you still close?'

'She died,' Tilly said.

Over tea in the bookstore café, Tilly told me how Melanie had battled polycystic kidney disease, the illness that had killed my aunt Elsie. 'It runs in the family,' said Tilly. 'You should have yourself checked.'

I nodded, not trusting myself to speak.

'I'm sorry to lay this on you,' she added. 'Melanie was ill for such a long time. We looked everywhere for you. We thought maybe you could help.'

'I was living in Sweden,' I said automatically, not comprehending her meaning. 'With my husband. I got married,' I explained.

'I guess that's why we couldn't find you. We didn't know your married name.' Tilly stared off into the distance. A bookstore employee was making a racket, stacking plastic chairs. 'We tried her aunts, but Rosemary was too sick. And Velva wasn't a match.'

'My aunts,' I corrected her. Tilly wasn't really part of the family; it was understandable that she'd get confused. 'They were Melanie's sisters.'

Tilly covered her mouth with her hand.

And so it was Tilly who told me that Melanie was not my aunt. She was my sister. Melanie, dying, had needed a kidney and the family had tried desperately to find me. They were certain that I'd be a match.

'I'm sorry,' Tilly said that day in the bookstore. 'We all assumed Peg had told you.'

But Peg, my mother, had not.

Melanie was born in August, the year my mother turned seventeen. A few years before, *Gone With the Wind* had opened in theatres, with Olivia de Havilland in the role of Melanie, a beautiful woman who also died young. It was my mother's favourite film. She saw it four times at the Regal Theatre. That was before she quit school and became a homebody, canning and cooking and helping my grandmother with the new baby.

I imagine a boy from a neighbouring farm, in love with my mother – a girl who lived for the movies, tall and red-haired and less shy than I'd been led to believe. Who was that boy, I wonder, and who was that girl? I have pieced together as much as I can. My mother and my aunts are gone now. There is nobody left to ask.

I remember Melanie that day in the Ag Hall, the odd gentleness in her voice as she admired our mother's quilt.

Is that your sister? the boy had asked me.

Kind of, Melanie answered with the smile I now think of as secretive. Did she know the truth then, or find out later? I missed my chance to ask her. I was in Sweden for three years with my husband. I wasn't here to help. ∎

THE HOUSE OF PROVISIONS

Lois Williams

In 1942, my mother would sit on the bus home from school and eat an imaginary sandwich. The journey on the 436 from Guildford to Addlestone took over an hour and was followed by a long walk from the bus stop to the house. To outwit her hunger she stared into the aisle of the bus and pictured a sandwich. She was fourteen. Her name was Patty Cockle.

She began in the usual way with a slice of bread and gave it a cuff of white crumbs where the knife had taken bite. To this she applied a film of margarine sprinkled with sugar, and then another slice of greased bread, the whole thing pressed down and cut in two and two diagonally – a dainty sandwich on a pretty china plate. She sat down at a table, on her own, savouring the yeasty tack of the bread on her palate, the grit-sweet melt of the sugar. By the time she got off the bus, she felt nourished, if not fed.

Soon after the armistice in 1945, an elderly man took a photograph of a street party in Weston Avenue. The frame is packed with faces, most of them children and youngsters. A few of the

From the box of bits: Patty and 'the errand boy' in 1960

mothers are there at the edges, the men still away. Their joy seems to fly out of the picture. They are young, apparently unscathed, and are wearing the Sunday best of folk who have one good set of clothes. My aunts and uncles are there, children on the shoulders of other children, babies in the arms of brothers and sisters. Patty is there. She's just turned seventeen and she smiles out of the crowd, her face cheeky and lovely.

It is hard to imagine she will also inhabit a life with me, for she seems fixed to this place, this time, to its bunting and jostling energy. She looks towards the camera and, it seems to me, through the lens into the chamber of mirrors and photographic plates where she appears upside down alongside her friends. She would enjoy the silliness of that, and its aptness, for the war has stood her on her head. I could be wistful and say she is looking to the future, and that the black box of the camera transforms before her gaze into the house she and my father come to live in, a place where I exist. But such a place is more than twenty years ahead and no one, not even Patty with her visionary's eye, can see that far. Although she knows my

father, she has yet to meet him again. Although he's been called up and gone, he's still the errand boy. I imagine, instead, the photograph was taken and the old man bantered into lifting up the cloth from the tripod, then lifting up the children to the squint to show them how it's done.

M y first recollection of looking at the world is a memory of jagged heads high up in a wall. They frightened me and made me cry. They weren't heads at all, I learned later, but broken panes in the windows of a warehouse. The glass was milky grey. Someone had thrown stones through to the black air inside. I saw the holes as heads, silhouettes with beaky mouths. My mother noticed how I cried each time we went along that street, so she took me home by another route and my fear vanished. Perhaps it stayed with the street and we left it there like a piece of litter. I like the idea that a fear could be emptied from a life as simply as turning out a pocket.

The memory of the windows is the only memory I have from the time before we lived in Norfolk. I think of it not as a memory of a place but as a marker of sight, a sort of eye test, which I suppose I failed not for lack of seeing but for want of knowing how else to see. It is also a memory of rescue: the fleeting pink coat sleeve passing my face when she reached down to pick me up, and the weather inside her voice, which was calm and mild. Back I went, into the sealed world of belonging not yet to myself, at home in my mother's world. Hers was a geology as layered and settled as the airing cupboard full of sheets and pillowslips. A world of soft things stacked deeply.

I remember in fragments the evening we came to the new house. Red buckled sandals on the car's back seat. My brother getting out to fetch a key. Copper light from stopping under trees late in the day in July. That light, that lantern feeling of waking up, is my first memory of being *in place* – of knowing we are somewhere and I am the youngest. Later, when the house and fields and sea are my familiars, our life there reels itself around me, turns me into a spool of a girl, gathering pictures, laying them down like fat.

The new house had many windows. At night because we lacked curtains the place was a lit stage, a diorama. I think of it now as it might have looked had you walked up the hill the first summer we lived there. A house glued to a sky, a plough of stars in a dark field. Sometimes a moon. Sometimes a goose across the moon, as in a nursery book. You would have seen us all together, man, woman, boy, girl, around the kitchen table with our plates and appetites. Had you stood outside with the breezes and the pollen trees, you would have seen us take up our scripts.

The man with the chisels is my father. He works at a trestle in the front room, sizing a plank for a hole in the floor. The joists show through like the bones of the house. When he kneels down to fit the new plank, my brother kneels with him and hammers it home. Piece by piece the ribs are covered. There's another hole at the far end of the room. My brother eases down into it and stands waist deep in floorboards, a flashlight in one hand, a wrench in the other. Then he lowers himself under the floor and is gone. I'm the small girl leaning round the door frame, not knowing Pete is very near, almost under my feet. I run to the kitchen where our mother is at the sink, pull at her skirt and lead her to the front room to show her this mystery. She wipes the suds from her hands as we go, by which time her son is there again.

Persons, things, appear and disappear, there and gone and there again like the tide and the gulls above the tide.

There are two neighbours, Aunt Marie and Mrs Pigeon, and when they come to the gate, the morning switches tune. Marie is the neighbour nearest in age to my mother. She has long black hair, tanned skin, and wears bright lipstick and high shoes that show her toes. Her feet are brown too. Sometimes her toenails match her lips. She is the deep orange rose that grows along the fence, familiar and striking. When Marie pops by, my mother gets out the tin of biscuits. They sit out on the back step with cups of tea while indoors the Burco boiler sloshes away at the washing. Marie is the one who prises my mother from her chores. They sit like schoolgirls chatting, Marie

holding her cigarette off to the side so the smoke won't blow on us. Time on the step feels large and entirely our own. *Promise me you won't start, Ducky,* she says, as if I understand.

Marie has a big dog, an Alsatian named Tosca, who goes with her like a shadow and whom she has trained for police work. He flattens out along the step and stays completely still. I sit beside him, trying to copy his stillness. His nose fascinates me. It makes me think of liquorice, and when the nostrils move in and out in their damp slight way I feel dizzy with the focus of watching him breathe. The tea is drunk down to the dregs, and then Marie says, *Let's see your leaves, Trish.* She makes my mother laugh in ways the others can't. I think she sees in her the street she's come from. She sees the scrubbed step, the scrubbed faces, slivers of soap they saved and melted down for making new.

Mrs Pigeon brings my mother jars of chutney and knitting patterns and pamphlets by Mary Baker Eddy. When she sees me she says, *Being good,* with an upturned lilt that means my goodness might be up for scrutiny. On the night of our arrival at the new house, she left for us a tray of sandwiches in the empty kitchen, a kindness my mother took to heart. I do not remember this meal so I imagine it as she might have found it: a melamine tray stacked with willow-pattern plates, a Tupperware box of ham and lettuce sandwiches. The crusts are missing from the bread. They will be on the bird feeder in Mrs Pigeon's garden. There are drinking glasses and a jug of water, paper serviettes. In the evening light, the kitchen's red ceiling makes the room feel short, and my mother ties a knot in her memory to have it painted first. She opens the box, arranges the sandwiches on the plates, and as her hands touch the bread the food becomes a meal from her own hand. She leads us back outside to the step, where we sit in the half-light like a family at roost, watching the sea.

We never do look like the family on the knitting patterns. If the girls are my size, they have freckles and a sister. If they have a brother, he's a baby or a twin. When there are fathers, there are also moustaches. None of the mothers has the N between her eyes.

It is my mother's special letter, the N. I see it there on her face one day, not long after we move to the house. I am swinging on the back door, hanging on the handle, arcing in and out of the kitchen while she works. *You're making a donkey of that door*, she says. *Get off. It's stubborn enough as it is.*

The door chafed on its frame. Already we'd learned to shove it to or heave it open. *To* and *open*, those are the words that go with the door. Open, and the garden enters the kitchen – finches and privet and a panel of light like a mopped floor. To, and the room is my mother's ship, her pans and spoons compasses pointing us to the table, where she pulls us back each night with full plates that we eat down to the sheen.

This particular day, she walks over to the door and holds it fast to stop me swinging. She isn't cross, she's amused – by my persistence, I suppose, and my belief in my own invisibility, as though I were just a voice asking and singing and not a body giving itself away. *Off your horse now, Neddy.* I look up into her face and see the faint crease between her eyes – faint and unmistakably the shape of an N. *You've got an N*, I say, touching her face. *It's all the frowning I do*, she says. *If you get off the door, it'll go away.*

It stays. I like that it is there, for it is part of her and part of the alphabet, and both are patterns I adore.

Mrs Pigeon comes by most days. She and my mother stand in the kitchen talking, and sometimes Mrs Pigeon sits down and rests her legs while my mother keeps on with the iron or the pastry. I don't remember the conversations for their news so much as for the way they teach me how to listen to a voice, for the story inside that goes by transparently but sometimes jumps up like a little dog behind a fence.

One day a man comes to the hill to dig a drain outside our house. By midday he has died and an ambulance taken him away. By a quarter past midday Mrs Pigeon is cooing at the kitchen door. Terrible pity, she says. Terrible shock. Not an old man at all. She sits down at the

table, my mother too, and the washing waits in the sink behind them. Saw him fall did you?

The man had chatted to my mother earlier that morning while she stood outside pinning up sheets. *Lovely sea*, he'd said. *A picture*, he'd said. *Wouldn't want to live anywhere else.* Later, when she went out to pin up the shirts, she found him dead in the grass. He was curled over like a dreaming man, the spade beside him sharp side down.

Fancy that, Mrs Pigeon says. *To go tidy like that.*

I think he went peacefully, my mother adds. She wants me not to be afraid. This is her way of being gentle, of seeking the good in things. She'd kept me inside in another part of the house until the ambulance closed its doors and left the hill quiet again.

There's only one journey, Mrs Pigeon begins, and I think of the ambulance with its winker on at the bottom of the road to show it is coming to our house. *There's one journey, one ticket.*

I think of the train to Ely and the scuff of carriage cloth behind my knees, the man with the hat who says, *All change*, and how there is one ticket, three trains, my mother with her raffia bag of sandwiches and gloves, and she knows which train to choose. When she points to the view outside, I see the spires and wheat and my reflection twinned in the glass. Looking joins me to the field, the canal, and later to the bricks and tunnels into London, where our journey stops at Liverpool Street, under the umbrella roof, the indoor sky with pigeons in its eaves.

The words, not the death, made me afraid. The digging man had said something and it had come true. He never did live anywhere else.

One journey, remember that. Being good.

My brother has the revival knack. He finds a dove knocked in the verge, carries it home inside his jacket. A cardboard box appears in the shed, holes in the top punched through with a pencil. I'm not allowed to look, not even to open the door. You'll frighten it, he says.

For three days he goes in and out. I hear him in there talking. He has the sort of patience a cat has. Had I found the dove, I would hold it too tight or too long, would open the box too many times. Pete waits. He puts crumbs in a jam-jar lid, water in a saucer. The bird heals itself and he releases it into the field, where it hops and flaps in the furrow and flies off.

My mother was not a gossip, so we seldom heard any stories of the doings of others since she never passed anything along. Gossip, like all business, is exchange. Her currency was food. Cakes, shortbread, pies with fluted crusts. She sent them out the door on plates or in tins, finished with a doily, to jumble sales, coffee mornings, any good cause that needed a sponge. It was her way of loving people, or perhaps her way of talking without words. Though I wished as I grew older that there were more conversations, fewer cakes. There was a time soon after I was eleven when something I didn't understand then began to grow alongside us. A quietness when I wanted answers. But it was so subtle, so quickly eclipsed by the doings of the house, that I couldn't grasp it. I remember coming in from school and being given a small slice of something sweet – often a piece of Bakewell tart, sometimes a fairy cake baked in a wax-paper frill, which I liked to peel away and scrape along my teeth. The mixture on the paper was cooked dark, almost bitter, from the extra oil. It was transporting, sweet and heavy. The flavour stayed in my mouth long after I'd left the table. She'd join me with her cup of tea and we'd sit there in the kitchen among ironing and the makings of the next meal. It was like sitting in a workshop. Everything there had a purpose. I realize now how pleased she was to see me after spending the day alone. I have sometimes thought her feeding me the cake was her way of making sure I would come home.

Patty Cockle was buxom. Or as her mother Mary put it, *well covered*; *developed*. Like a secret or a photograph. In a better-off family they might have said she was curvaceous or Rubenesque or some word you could say without seeing the quotation marks

winking at you. The way they saw it, her skinny sisters and the two boys, there was simply more of Patty than there was of the others. More and sooner. Mary put her daughter's solidity down to studying at the technical school – not the books part of things but the PE, the shinning up ropes and the free midday dinner.

Patty was there on a trade scholarship to study Homecraft & Housewifery. She got a free meal, a bus pass and a uniform allowance, and when she left the house in the morning and you saw her walking along Station Road in her blue, pleated skirt and banded hat, you'd not know she was a girl who imagined a sandwich on the bus and went home to a family of eight with three beds and a cot between them. When Mary looked at Patty she saw her plump and rosy girl, her second child and, when she thought about it, her understudy, for Patty was a little mother, good with babies, good with patience. And sometimes when she looked, Mary felt she was glimpsing through lace curtains a well-furnished front room, and behind it a house of provisions: boiled beef, treacle pudding, the whole larder.

Patty Cockle was a believer.

She had great faith in the chemistry of culinary production, especially the agency of the egg to rise a cake, enrich a bread, and the power of sour milk to make scones of the lightest consistency. When Patty stood at her workbench in the technical school, her hand around the egg, she knew she held lightning. The cracked egg was a cracked sky letting out its yellow vigour. And the recipes she learned by heart – well, they were prayers of an earthly kind, practical miracles, which, if she found it hard to believe in God, she could follow instead. They would lead her back to the feeling she loved of making things – and from there it wasn't so hard to remember she'd been made, in an earthly way but with, she was sure in hope, a grain of the divine somewhere in her. Perhaps it was dissolved into her like a speck of salt in a pickling brine. Perhaps it was a whole thing, a peppercorn or a clove. She was fairly sure it would be pungent, flavouring, strong enough to think about.

Patty also believed in the 'wide net' tradition, or as she preferred to think of it (not liking the idea of a thing being trapped), the 'wide street', the 'avenue of faith': there were many paths to God. Jesus was a sturdy step, the one she'd happened to put her feet on and he hadn't tripped her up yet, so she'd kept walking. Patty's sister, Peggy, believed in Helena Rubinstein and she had the beautiful half-moon cuticles to show for it.

Patty's hands were not beautiful but practical. She had a cook's short nails and a cook's fingers, able to take the nip of heat from plates straight from the oven. She could carry a casserole to a table without thinking twice about it, her mind already on the dishing up, the tucking in. She also had the blue veins that wouldn't stay flat. They meandered down from her wrists like rivers in spate. She had always disliked their obviousness until the day she'd come home from school excited by the news the teacher had given her: Patty had artisan's hands. She hadn't known what the word meant, but it sounded wonderfully important and not poor at all, and it had the word *art* in it, which pleased her no end. She held up her hands, admiring the straight-backed thumb, straight all the way to the top, a thumb with good posture, as good as Peggy's. *I've got artisan's hands Mam,* she'd told Mary. *What does it mean?* And Mary told her it meant she'd be working hard all her life. She took her daughter's hand in her own and stroked the back of it. *But this,* she touched the blue part, *is the blood of the kings of Ireland a-galloping through your veins.*

Horses in her blood. Sometimes she would feel them stomping and snorting in the quiet stable of her heart. Which is how, when my father the errand boy came home from Malaya in 1949, all skin and grief and sallow as dripping, she felt nudged to visit him. She took a cake.

Pete was the one who gave me my name. They were going to call me Grace; my father liked the name and my mother is a Christian. A beautiful name, a syllable of mist or kindness it sounds to me now, but it must have sounded old to his child's ear, a grandmother's

name, full of aprons and hatpins. The story goes that when they brought me home from hospital, he ran across the street to the Lee boys and Gareth Harris and Nigel Lemeseure and told them he had a sister. *I've got a sister called Lois,* he said. And that was that.

I remember learning prayers with my mother.

The evening is still pale outside. Its grey light, pigeon light I think of it, chips under the edge of the curtain, a soft hammer. In other rooms, the day is continuing. Another floor is being mended, my brother up and down with his torch again. My mother sits on the child's chair beside my bed and strokes the hair back from my face. *It's like talking aloud,* she says, *but you can say it in your head if you like.* I fold my hands and close my eyes and she gives me the words: *God bless Mummy, God bless Dadda, God bless Peter, God bless Lois…*

I wonder why her name goes first, because when she dishes up the dinner she always goes last, and if there's anything a bit scraggy she'll take it for her plate instead of giving it to us. But here she is first, before my father even.

I can say the words inside my head but I'm always surprised when I come to my name, to hear myself as someone outside myself yet still inside my head. It feels like a spiralling kaleidoscope, as if I am rushing into my head's blue centre, so I say them aloud and my name becomes another girl, like me but not exactly me. A girl on a knitting pattern maybe or a girl outside in the evening, not listening, not called in yet.

The year I turn seven, Marie leaves with Tosca and Reg. They go to South Africa to own a garage. The step stays but I don't think my mother sits on it again. Pete says, *How could they do that, be owners in South Africa.* I don't know why he says what he says. Some words in some combinations make everyone go quiet.

One day Mrs Pigeon tells my mother, *It's not right for a girl to be poorly so often. If the soul's right the body follows.*

It's her throat, my mother tells her. *Her soul's all right.* But I could see she was hurt.

T he Wash is a place of shifting light. Some moments the horizon is hidden in rain. Another moment the coast of Lincolnshire tips up forty miles away. When the tide pulls out on a clear day, I feel as if I'm seeing the land at its most primitive. The Wash becomes a vast bronze expanse, a sunken desert, and the trees and spires on the other side rise out of it as spined creatures might once have risen from prehistoric mud. On days like this, when the sea is gone for the afternoon, the far strand of Lincolnshire seems deceptively near, merely a stroll across the sand.

When, recently, I asked my mother why here, why this house was the one they chose, she answered that she and my father had thought they would be able to take care of it into their retirement. It was an almost one-storey house, a bungalow the estate agent called it, or, as the previous owners had thought of it, a sort-of-croft. They'd even given it a name plate on the gate, Ulverscroft. Rickety and oddly laid out inside, but with a lovely view of the sea. As a child I wanted to know who Ulver was, or where it was, but it or he was imaginary. They had made it up because they missed the mountains.

I had always thought the word *bungalow* was ugly, beginning with *bung* and ending in *low*, making a house of stoppered sorrows before you even walked in the door. My mother says she had liked very much the carrstone three-storey house set back from a road in a village near a town, but she and my father felt it would be beyond them when they grew old. Too tall. I don't think it occurred to them that they might move again once they'd bought a house, nor that they might get help in looking after things later in life. They were workers all their lives, which bred a self-sufficiency not only of provision but of thought. So, in their early forties, with their half-grown boy and their late-in-the-day-too-late-for-another girl, they bought a house they could live in for the foreseeable and for the eventual.

The photograph of the street party came down from their attic in a box of bits in 1993. I'd come home from Pittsburgh, from a failed marriage, too much of a stunned animal to think. One afternoon my father brought down boxes: *See if there's anything in there worth*

looking at, he said. It was a gift of distraction. He must have known. Lives other than my own to be with.

There is an afterthought from near the beginning that belongs, I think, to this place: my mother would never have let us drop litter on Jagged Head Street, or anywhere for that matter. She was the sort of person to tread lightly and to 'leave no trace' long before they started printing that saying on signs in forests. She had a strong sense of obligation towards public beauty. One day she walked up to the window of a car that had stopped for ice creams along the coast road through the village. The driver had tipped out his ashtray on to the pavement. *Why are you doing that?* she asked. *I don't want it,* he said. *And nor do we,* she returned. She picked up the mess and handed it back to him.

That was her way, to begin with a question. ■

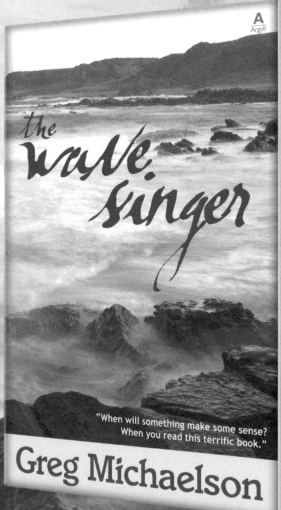

"If you challenge the song
 then you challenge our stability"

A rare debut
novel.

Publication
coincides with
the UK release
of Hercules
Mandarin's
new single,
The Wave
Singer.

the wave singer

"When will something make some sense?
When you read this terrific book."

Greg Michaelson

ARGYLL ✣ PUBLISHING
www.thewavesinger.co.uk • August 2008 •
£8.99 pbk • 9781906134273 •

GRANTA

THE MAGAZINE OF NEW WRITING

Make a gift of good writing with a Granta subscription
– fiction, reportage, memoir, biography and photography four times a year

Buy a twelve-month subscription for a friend and receive, with our compliments, a *Granta* special-edition **MOLESKINE**® notebook

Subscribe online at **www.granta.com**
or by **Freephone 0500 004 033**
or fill in the **coupon overleaf** and send to us

'With each new issue, Granta *enhances its reputation for presenting, in unequalled range and depth, the best contemporary writers in journalism and fiction.'*
SUNDAY TIMES

Gift subscription offer: take out an annual subscription as a gift and you will also receive a complimentary *Granta* special edition **MOLESKINE**® notebook

GIFT SUBSCRIPTION 1

Address:

TITLE: INITIAL: SURNAME:

ADDRESS:

POSTCODE:

TELEPHONE:

EMAIL:

GIFT SUBSCRIPTION 2

Address:

TITLE: INITIAL: SURNAME:

ADDRESS:

POSTCODE:

TELEPHONE:

EMAIL:

YOUR ADDRESS FOR BILLING

TITLE: INITIAL: SURNAME:

ADDRESS:

POSTCODE:

TELEPHONE: EMAIL:

NUMBER OF SUBSCRIPTIONS	DELIVERY REGION	PRICE	SAVINGS
☐	UK	£29.95	32%
☐	Europe	£35.95	18%
☐	Rest of World	£39.95	10%

I would like my subscription to start from: All prices include delivery

☐ the current issue ☐ the next issue GRANTA IS PUBLISHED QUARTERLY

PAYMENT DETAILS

☐ I enclose a cheque payable to '*Granta*' for £_____ for _____ subscriptions to *Granta*

☐ Please debit my ☐ MASTERCARD ☐ VISA ☐ AMEX for £_____ for _____ subscriptions

NUMBER ☐☐☐☐ ☐☐☐☐ ☐☐☐☐ ☐☐☐☐ SECURITY CODE ☐☐☐

EXPIRY DATE ☐☐ / ☐☐ SIGNED _____ DATE _____

☐ Please tick this box if you would like to receive special offers from *Granta*
☐ Please tick this box if you would like to receive offers from organizations selected by *Granta*

Please return this form to: **Granta Subscriptions, PO Box 2068, Bushey, Herts, WD23 3ZF, UK, call Freephone 0500 004 033** or go to **www.granta.com**

Please quote the following promotion code when ordering online: GBIUK103

SOLDIERS

Living with British troops in
Afghanistan and Iraq

Photographs by Lalage Snow

The text that accompanies the pictures is taken from letters
written by Leanne Dixon to her husband Corporal John Dixon,
who is serving with Number 2 Company, Ist Battalion
Coldstream Guards. They live in Sunderland, with their son,
J, and have been married for three years.

Forward Operating Base, Arnhem, Helmand Province, Afghanistan

'Just thought I would send you a letter to let you know how much I miss you and want you to be home.'

'J is still being
naughty, though,
so you will have
to put him in
his place when
you come home.
Not long now,
twenty-eight
days. Woo!'

Lt Malcolm Deizel Job's shelves, FOB Arnhem, Helmand Province, Afghanistan

'My slimming pills are really working. I can feel I have lost weight on them which is good, plus I have been stocking up on tanning products as I don't want to look like a milk bottle next to you like I did when you came back from Iraq.'

Camp Bastion, Helmand Province, Afghanistan

'I hope you are okay. Did you get all those photos? What do you think of my new hair colour? Better than the blonde?'

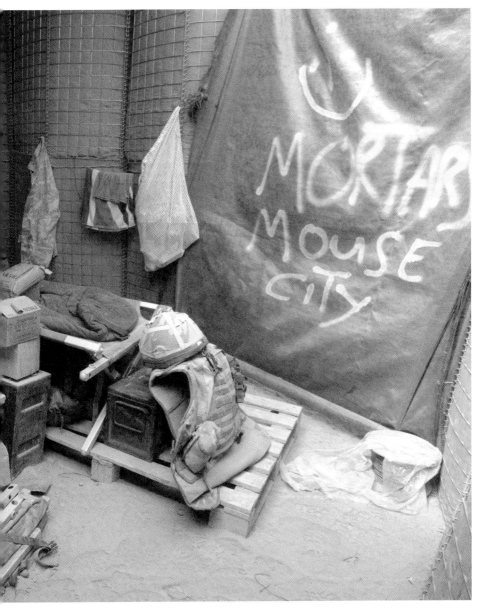

Mortar Platoon's living quarters, FOB Arnhem, Helmand Province, Afghanistan

'My Nana's funeral was a good send-off for her. She had so many people there which was good. The most upsetting bit about it was when her coffin turned up outside the house. It was awful. I really could have done with you there.'

Camp Bastion, Helmand Province, Afghanistan

Camp Bastion, Helmand Province, Afghanistan

'I baked cakes with J today, he was so happy – just a shame you weren't there – tidied the house today, too, as it was a right mess.'

'I had a dream
last night that
you got hurt.
It wasn't nice
and I woke
up crying.'

Guardsman Allwood, left, and Corporal Mayo, FOB Arnhem, Helmand, Afghanistan

Corporals Richardson and Wall, Camp Bastion, Helmand Province, Afghanistan

'When you get this letter you are going to be mad at me. I have something to tell you. Please don't shout and scream at me because it is my problem and I will sort it out on my own. I have maxed my Visa card again.'

Welfare tent, Camp Delta, Basra Air Station, Iraq, Christmas Day, 2007

'I know these letters are supposed to make you smile, but I am really down at the minute. It is all the stuff going on over there – I heard about it in the news. I think it's because I haven't heard your voice for a few days that I just need someone to talk to.'

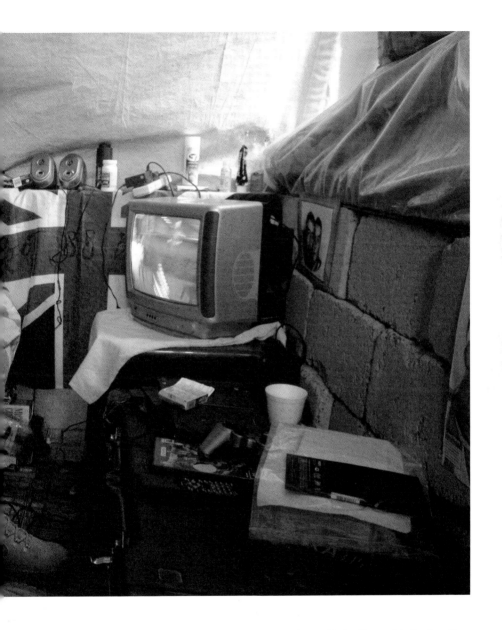

Corporal White, Camp Delta, Basra Air Station, Iraq

'Like I said the other day, it is killing us as a family. I just want us to live normal lives, just the three of us. It's not long until you are home so you can either scream when you get this letter or scream at me when you come home. I would prefer it if you did it when you come home.'

Camp Delta, Basra Air Station, Iraq

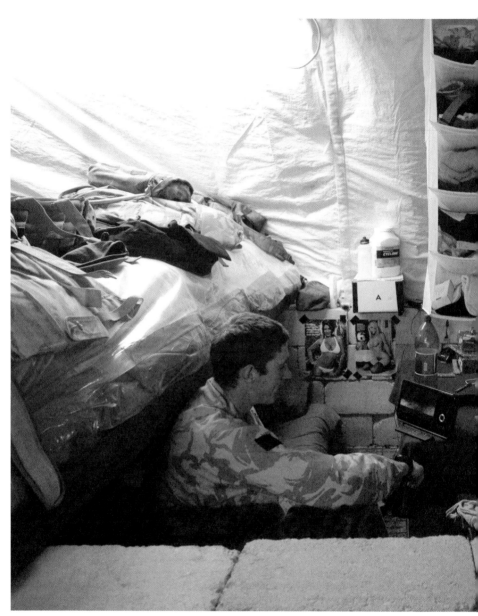

Camp Delta, Basra Air Station, Iraq

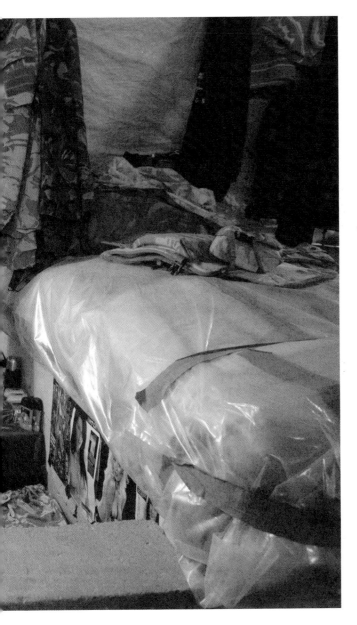

'I can't wait to
see you just to
have a cuddle
from you and
for you to tell
me you are okay
and everything
is going to be
all right.'

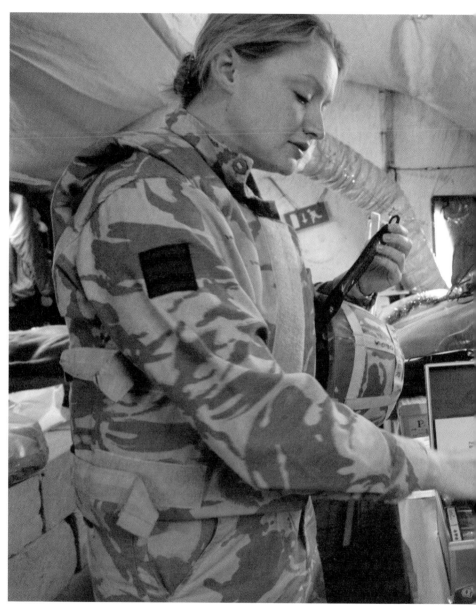
Captain Mel Fletcher opens her welfare box from the Queen, Camp Delta, Iraq

'J has been as good as gold but I had to walk to the shop with him in his Power Ranger outfit as he refused to take it off. Everyone thought it was cute. I couldn't stop laughing.'

Corporal Lal, Camp Delta, Basra Air Station, Iraq

'Just got four letters through the post from you. The things you write just make me bubble and cry but it is so nice to see you feel like that as you never express your feelings in person. I had better go now as J needs changing.'

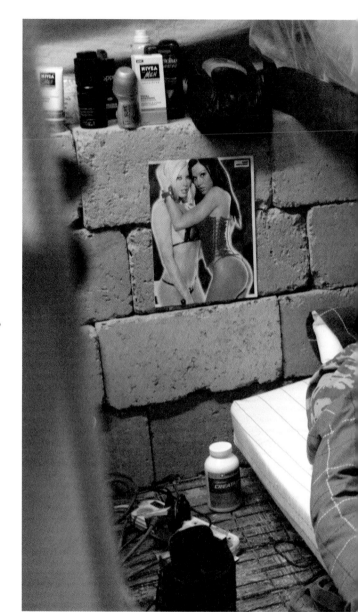

'P.S. What do
you want for
your birthday?'

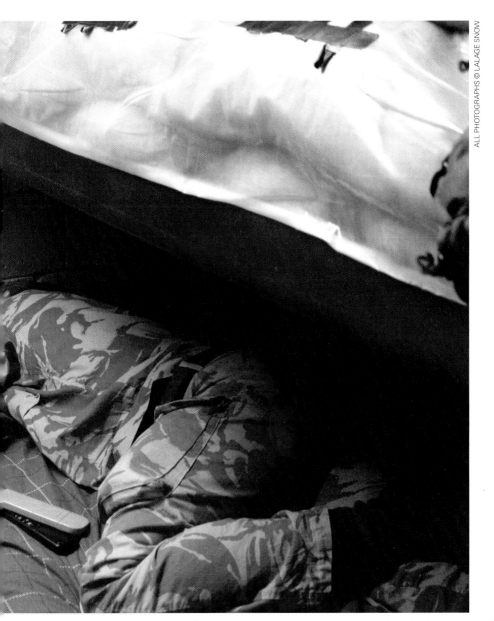

Camp Delta, Basra Air Station, Iraq

RSC
ROYAL
SHAKESPEARE
COMPANY

LONDON SEASON 08-09
WILTON'S MUSIC HALL

The RSC returns to London with two exciting new plays in 'London's most beautiful lost theatre' DAILY MAIL

THE TRAGEDY OF THOMAS HOBBES
By Adriano Shaplin
WED 12 NOV – SAT 6 DEC 08

A provocative and experimental journey to a time when science was theatre and philosophy was faith

THE CORDELIA DREAM
By Marina Carr
A new RSC commission
THU 11 DEC 08 – SAT 10 JAN 09

A razor-sharp dissection of a stifling and shattered relationship

TICKETS FROM £15

RSC TICKET HOTLINE
0844 800 1118
(NO BOOKING FEE, CALLS FROM BT LANDLINE COST 5P PER MINUTE)

BOOK ONLINE
www.rsc.org.uk
(NO BOOKING FEE)

The work of the RSC Literary Department is generously supported by THE DRUE HEINZ TRUST
The RSC's New Work is generously supported by CHRISTOPHER SETON ABELE on behalf of the ARGOSY FOUNDATION

> accenture

WILTON'S
The City's hidden stage

ARTS COUNCIL ENGLAND

Subscription offer: take out an annual subscription to *Granta* and receive a complimentary *Granta* special edition **MOLESKINE**® notebook

YOUR ADDRESS FOR DELIVERY

Your address:

TITLE: INITIAL: SURNAME:

ADDRESS:

POSTCODE:

TELEPHONE:

EMAIL:

Billing address if different:

TITLE: INITIAL: SURNAME:

ADDRESS:

POSTCODE:

TELEPHONE: EMAIL:

NUMBER OF SUBSCRIPTIONS	DELIVERY REGION	PRICE	SAVINGS	DIRECT DEBIT PRICES	SAVINGS
☐	UK	£29.95	32%	**£24.95**	**43%**
☐	Europe	£35.95	18%	**£32.95**	**29%**
☐	Rest of World	£39.95	10%	**£35.95**	**18%**

I would like my subscription to start from:

☐ the current issue ☐ the next issue

All prices include delivery

GRANTA IS PUBLISHED QUARTERLY

PAYMENT DETAILS

☐ I enclose a cheque payable to '*Granta*' for £_____ for _____ subscriptions to *Granta*

☐ Please debit my ☐ MASTERCARD ☐ VISA ☐ AMEX for £_____ for _____ subscriptions

NUMBER ☐☐☐☐ ☐☐☐☐ ☐☐☐☐ ☐☐☐☐ SECURITY CODE ☐☐☐

EXPIRY DATE ☐☐ / ☐☐ SIGNED _____ DATE _____

Instruction to your Bank or building society to pay Direct Debit

DIRECT Debit

TO THE MANAGER:

(BANK OR BUILDING SOCIETY NAME)

ADDRESS:

POSTCODE:

ACCOUNT IN NAME(S) OF:

SIGNED: DATE:

BANK/BUILDING SOCIETY ACCOUNT NUMBER

☐☐☐☐☐☐☐☐

SORT CODE

☐☐ ☐☐ ☐☐

Instructions to your Bank or building society Please pay Granta Publications Direct Debits from the account detailed on this instruction subject to the safeguards assured by the Direct Debit Guarantee. I understand that this instruction may remain with Granta and, if so, details will be passed electronically to my Bank/ building society.

Banks and building societies may not accept Direct Debit instructions from some types of account

ORIGINATOR'S IDENTIFICATION

9	1	3	1	3	3

☐ Please tick this box if you would like to receive special offers from *Granta*
☐ Please tick this box if you would like to receive offers from organizations selected by *Granta*

Please return this form to: **Granta Subscriptions, PO Box 2068, Bushey, Herts, WD23 3ZF, UK, call Freephone 0500 004 033** or go to **www.granta.com**

Please quote the following promotion code when ordering online: GBIUK103

HIGH TABLE

Craig Raine

The senior fellow's semi-shaven Adam's apple
shifty on the frayed collar of his check shirt.

Massaging gold,
thumb and index finger
soothe his signet ring.
An osculation. A frig. On his little finger.

Impatient. He pushes back his cuff,
consults the scratched three-quarter face.
And catches the butler's professionally placid eye.
'We can't wait any longer for the chaplain.'

The chaplain is on her knees,

her trousered knees, gowned, dog-collared,
pushing a prepuce back, down,
with finger and thumb.

If you look,
you can just make out
the label (Russell and Bromley)
pricing her pair of black Oxfords.
There. See. At the pale pristine instep.

Anointing the glans
with its glycerine.

A hand on her head,
blessing and forcing.

Catching the chrism on her tongue.
Two small drops. Quick. Not copious.

On her feet.

And running.
Now diagonally across the quad,
caught in the commotion of her gown,
plucked, enveloped, billowing black.

The inescapable smoke of her gown,
streaming, rips and tears at the sleeves.
Running.
The smack of her shoes on the wet flags
rhyming in the Cloisters.
A squash court of echoes,
intense rally of echoes.

Taking the steps to Hall
two at a time.

Steady. Still her breathing. Stroll.
Pull the points of her waistcoat down.

The gavel is poised. Brought down.
The butler draws back the chair
at the head of high table.
The senior fellow rises. The fellows follow, stand.
A long Latin grace
leaves the lips of the senior scholar
gracelessly, a gabble of echoes.

See the seams of the servants' skirts,
the trouser seams, and the thumbs
at attention along the line of each seam.

The chaplain freeze-framed
in the body of the Hall.
Her dog collar's dim smile,
grey-white sperm.

Candle flames curtsey and stretch.
Relax and flex. Flex and relax.

Amen.

* * * * *

Exterior. Traffic lights. Daytime.
The next day.

Peterhouse reflected, curved
across a crash helmet's black visor.

Gauntlets gripping
the high handlebars of a chopped hog.

The right hand
flexing, relaxing,
retaining the revs,
the engine's excitement,

then roaring away
with open throttle
down Trumpington Street
as the traffic lights change.

* * * * *

Heaving the Harley-Davidson
onto its stand. Resistance, weight. Flex
and relax.

Planted. In the kitchen quad.
Bling of chrome. The tyre treads
plaited like corn rows.

Gauntlets tight under his armpit.
Fingers fidget with the helmet fastening.

Towards you, towards you,
folds of leather
relax and flex
as the crotch comes into close up.

* * * * *

Serried on the tabletop,
dull with Goddard's Silver Dip,
brightness breathed on, slandered,
clouded, smeared, opaque,
silver salvers, silver sugar dredgers,
candelabras, candlesticks, teapots.

Each item
stagnant as a stage-mirror.

Silver cutlery is kept sheathed
in pocketed baize scrolls
which tie with tabs.
Twelve items per scroll.
They open out like cloth tool kits.

Thrown on the table like a trophy,
the black helmet,
then the gauntlets' challenge.

Gauntleted herself in pink rubber gloves,
Angelika hardly looks up
from the fork she is frigging clean.

Then she slowly caresses
the curve of a candelabra,
the rise of a spout.
With gangrened fingertips.

Nylon z-zzzzz-zzzzzip unzipped
like a Yamaha
flicking through corners,
going through gears.
He sheds his leathers,
naked under them.

For a moment, he is Marsyas,
upper body hanging, peeled
to the pubic bone.

Scrotum sways as he shrugs out of his leathers,
shaking a leg,
shaking the other leg free.

Stands in the kitchen dusk,
clean as a candle,
whiter than wax,
a source of light.

There are two things to notice:
the scooped curves
where his buttocks tense,
the different, tightening browns
of his furrow, foreskin and balls.

Then he becomes the butler.

Coaxing cufflinks into the crack
of each starched cuff, yes,
cramming buttons through crevices.
Glances into the mirror,
and folds down his collar,
trapping his black tie.

Adjusts the silk: a slither
of changing length and width
alive in the fold of his collar.

Wrapping the slick round the slack,
feeding silk into itself.
Tightening. Tightening.
Working the solid knot
into the V.

Then the throb of buttons
along the length of his brocaded waistcoat,
mother-of-pearl
quick under his fingers,
one after one after one…

He studies his face in the mirror.
Neutral. Fair haired. Forty.
Smoothing his eyebrows with spit.

Angelika still at the kitchen table,
masturbating a tablespoon,
mechanically, getting a glitter.

They haven't exchanged a word.

* * * * *

In Hall, the servants are laying high table.
On a simple piece of polished wood,
napkins like amulets, tumblers,
two wine glasses per place.

Cold, clear jugs of cubist water,
iced with angles and semi-opaque planes.

The pattern of cutlery,
orderly as surgical instruments,
or a percussionist's frieze.
Or the repeat in a Mexican blanket.

An elaborately chased silver-gilt
seventeenth-century kissing cup
will captivate the quarter-tones
of candlelight.

* * * * *

Interior. The Butler's pantry.

He angles the corkscrew
and insinuates its length

(mice-squeaks
mute to obscene murmur)

deep in the Cantenac-Brown,
a decent Margaux for a Guest Night.
Better than decent. Almost indecent.
3ième cru classé, 1994. Perfect for drinking.

The cork resists, then
comes, with a little gasp.

He passes the drawn cork,
dark as a Tampax, under his nostrils.

Winds out the corkscrew,
begins on the next. Scoring
the soft heavy foil,
winding it off.

The camp, pantomime smooch
of further corks coming out.

* * * * *

Angelika leans to her left,
to balance the weight of the wines
in the crook of her arm.
Four bottles to each wicker basket.

At the base of her biceps
(bulging, the size of a Kiwi fruit)
two visible tendons.

On her tiny hard muscle,
a definite grey-blue vein,
slightly twisted.

A kink in the vein
that fascinates the eye.

But we are behind her behind:
its altering outline in her tight black trousers.

Its fluent flesh,
repeating a ritual.

Continuity. Change.
Weight. Counter-weight.
Simple scales.
The slow tip, the languid rise.

Simple scales
in slow motion.
Practising perfection.
Left hand. Then right hand.
Now both hands together.

Mechanics as music.
Its mystery obvious
and impossible to analyse.

See its rise and fall,
flex and relax,
and fail to finish your sentence

for the singing, the singing,
melody flooding your mind.

Angelika can interrupt
the Regius Professor of Divinity
talking to the Regius Professor of Ecclesiastical History.

* * * * *

Thursday. Guest Night.

Neither Regius Professor is dining tonight.

The college fields
its President, the President's wife,

two bachelor heterosexual dons,
Bennett, Computing Science,
Ainsworth, English (Early Modern);

the Newton Professor of Physics.
(Rasmus Petersen, her guest, has won a Nobel Prize,
for work on genetics.)

Alan Howard, the Music Fellow,
a cripple, whose guest
(there are only two guests)
is the writer Ralph Clifford.

Finally, Farley, the Russian don.

Nine. A modest midweek total.

(One of the waiters,
out of Wisconsin, out of funds,
is doing his doctorate on Wittgenstein.)

* * * * *

Sir Alan, the President,
is already fortified
before he lifts to the light
(two streamers of bubbles,
twin towers of tiny fish eggs
perfectly balanced)
his second glass of champagne:
'Wonderful stuff, alcohol.
Over-the-counter sodium pentothal.
I used to be a chemist,'
he explains to Clifford in the Common Room.
'Tell me you used to be a writer.'

'I write fiction. Novels. Short stories.'
Clifford is famous, internationally known.
Famous enough to ignore
the President's feigned ignorance.
Also forewarned. He knows what to expect.

'Not recently, I hear.
I hear you're blocked.'
Booze: the President's problem
takes the form of 'candour'.
(Call it deliberate rudeness.)

Otherwise the problem is invisible.

Howard, the crippled music fellow,
looks much drunker than the President:
toppling on his two sticks
coming across the rucked kilim
to rescue his guest.

(There used to be a wooden toy,
a leggy foal, say, or a calf,
with limbs in elasticated sections:
alert, erect, poised on a plinth,
it detumesced
when you pressed a spring.

Then sprang up again.
Howard is poised when parked
– those steepled, attentive hands –
dishevelled, disintegrating when he walks.
'Left in the lurch.' Howard's joke.)

* * * * *

Ainsworth (English, Early Modern)
sports a single silver earring
through a fleshy lobe,
shirt-tail outside his trousers,
a casual, meticulously maintained,
two-day growth of beard,
rings on his thumbs:
a self-conscious semiology

that signals
one unpedantic pedagogue,
unpredictable, exciting, *young.*

He is 30 and explaining,
not for the first time,
the etymology of 'insincere'.

Apparently, the Latin for 'wax' is 'cera'
and the Latin for 'without' is 'sine'.
'When the Romans bought a marble sculpture,
you see, the flaws were concealed with wax.
So a flawless piece of marble
was 'sincere', without wax.'

The President contemplates his wine
and interrupts:
'Dr Ainsworth, spare us your party piece.
You're like a character in Chekhov.
A minor character. A schoolmaster
restricted to one rigmarole.
Whose wife is being swived
by the local landowner.
The only alternative to etymology.
Bloody good Margaux.'

Ainsworth irrepressible, erroneous:
'The etymology of "swived"
is from the Anglo-Saxon "swinken".
Which means to work.
"Swinken" is a strong verb, so…'

The President:
'A minor character,
but a major irritation.'

Ainsworth confides to Clifford:
'We endure the President's impatience
patiently. Sometimes High Table
resembles Out Patients at the Fullbourn.'

Ainsworth pleased with his playful syllables.
He will repeat them.
Like a minor character in Chekhov.

'The Fullbourn is a mental hospital.'
Footnote for the benefit of Clifford.

* * * * *

Rasmus Petersen is bald.
Freckled as a curlew's egg.
Nearly 70 now, he refuses to believe
his best work behind him:
'Once we isolate those genes
that cause the undesirable effects…'

The Newton Professor of Physics,
his host, Pamela Johansson,
interrupts –

an irritated lesbian,
she has heard it before

–confides to Petersen
that Angelika (or Angelika's arse)
should have an honorary fellowship
for sterling service to the college.

Nods in its direction.

Its gravitas,
its wag.

The Nobel Laureate,
stopped in his tract.

* * * * *

Lady Charlotte, Charlie Rowth,

the President's wife,
with tumbleweed hair
and misbuttoned blouse
(the dangling brooch, upside down,
Charlie's concession to evening wear)
extends her filthy fingernails
to say:

'If it wasn't for *these*,'

(across her chest,
her gardening hands
like gardening gloves,
clutch, but fail to cover,
her extensive breasts)

'I'd be a tight head prop.
Or a lock forward.
If it wasn't for these.'

Pamela Johansson speaks across High Table:
'Charlie, you do know, don't you,
that a women's rugger team exists?'

* * * * *

Interior. SCR lavatories.

Mahogany seats. Splash back.
The urinal flushes:
an awkward, injured fan,
as if someone had opened
a shaken soda water.
Farley, the Fellow in Russian,
is showing his breasts to Bennett,
Computing don.

Explaining the areolas.
'The miracle of oestrogen.
You want them to be right.'

He cups the little tits
in his hands. Looks in the mirror.

Bennett thinks:
but your hands will always be male.

He says:

'Angelika better look to her laurels.'

And Farley:
'Still harping on his daughter.'

* * * * *

Interior. Candlelight. Common Room.
Silver liquid in light.
Small laboratory of wines:
more Margaux, port, sauterne, an Alsace Riesling.
A shingle beach of nuts.
The fools' gold of Ferrero Rocher.
That ole Black Magic.
A ruined ziggurat of cherries.

Ainsworth is explaining
innuendo in Laurence Sterne.

Turning up the volume of his ring,
he lectures his glass of Fonseca 65:
'Behind the simpering pretence
of sensibility, Larry the Lad –

deliberate dirty-mindedness.
(I quote the other Lawrence,
D H, David Herbert, Bertie Lawrence
on Jimmy Joyce's *Ulysses*).'

The President to Ralph Clifford,
an audible aside:
'Dr Ainsworth is on first-name terms
with every author on the syllabus.
As we address the college servants.
Claret helps.'

Ainsworth, unabashed, uninterrupted:
'deliberate dirty-mindedness
which defies our censure.
Why? Because we are complicit.
All innuendo requires autocomplete.
Which shows we're made of Sterner stuff.'

The President's migraine voice:
'Something he prepared earlier.'

'In *A Sentimental Journey*,
he was the Graham Norton of his day,

comedian also Queer Theorist.
"The Theorist as Artist":
(I adapt from Oscar the intersexualist.)
Nothing he could not sexualise:
quills and inkwells, thimbles, gloves,
gloves, my God, the neck of a purse,
threading a needle. The old in-out.'

The President confides to the tablecloth:
'Ainsworth, you could blight Angelika's arse.'

In fact, Ainsworth has it in mind –
Angelika's arse.

* * * * *

Rasmus on his hobby-horse:
'so, via genetics, the genius of Mozart.'
He wards off interruption
with a palsied hand.

But Alan Howard intervenes:
'Yes, the genius of Mozart.
True, he transcribed Allegri's "Miserere"
after hearing it once in the Sistine Chapel.
Once, and once only. Aged 14.
A famous feat of musical memory.
Generally designated "genius".'

Howard lifts his own pale hand.

And pushes away the pale china plate
with his other fine fingers.
On it two tiny planets –
his still life of cherry stones.

'But, Rasmus, the autograph of K 385
records a clutch of second-thoughts,
of hesitations, alternatives.
He composed, corrected, made mistakes,
Corrected. Thought twice, improved.
We can see him thinking the music through.
It wasn't dictation from the deity.'

Mozart's tendency to 'take dictation':
light-fingered virtuoso at the keyboard…
Howard's head,
the head of a Hollywood star,

remembers (but keeps in reserve)
Muzio Clementi and *Die Zauberflöte*.

Rasmus responds:
'Exactly. Exactly. I agree. Exactly *that*.
By engineering to *improve* the DNA.
To correct the chromosome
and eliminate mistakes.
We screen for abnormalities.
The gene for, for example, homosexuality.'

'What about screening for baldness?'
Pamela Johansson *lesbian ad hominem*.
'That's pretty undesirable.'

And Howard:
'I accept I differ from the norm.
Impossible with spina bifida
to walk with ease.
Lumbar procedures
keep hydrocephalus at bay.
This isn't merely tiresome.'

He falters.
Wondering whether to risk
his reputation for wry urbanity.

'I am too ashamed
to take my clothes off…
even for a prostitute.'

Sex. Two cherry stones.
The meagreness.

And a line of George Herbert
like heartache in his head:
'Love bade me welcome…'

Love. The heart in free fall,
giving up the ghost to gravity,
safe in someone's arms.

Close to tears
which he keeps from his voice:
'But I wouldn't want
to be weeded out. By anyone.'

* * * * *

Interior. The Butler's pantry.
Angelika leans her hands and arse
along the edge of his desk.

Talking down
to the Butler sprawled in his chair.
Tie an off-duty, off-centre Y.

She says:
'He's a fantastic writer.
I've read everything he's written.
My Auntie Mary, *The Love Bird*,
A Table for Three. *Chinese Chopsticks*
is one of my favourite books.
I have to speak to him.
Taiga's a set-text.'

The Butler,
licking the length of a roll-up:
'Go ahead. Feel free.
But I wouldn't if I were you.
It's not the servant thing – '
Zippo poised
then lit with practised expertise –
a Karate move. Chop-chop.
And as swiftly extinguished.
'College is too full of cant
to put you in your place.
I just don't like the look of him.
He's got those actors' eyes –
always making eye contact.
You only fill his fucking glass
and you get the comether.'

Angelika:
'You're jealous.
It's just my beautiful backside.'

The Butler:
'Listen. *I* pour the wine. Not you.
Man or woman. Makes no difference.'
He stares, unseeing, at the desk. Remembering.
Depth of focus. Quiet intensity. *Italics*.
'Something extra in the way they look.
Hitler had it. Clinton. Blair. You feel *seen*.
And it's automatic. Pure technique.

You know when someone gives your hand a squeeze?
They do it, only with their eyes.
And it's only the eyes.'

Angelika:
'He's a great writer.'

The Butler,
forking his hair with his fingers,
yawning like a tragic mask:
'Suit yourself.
You always do.'

And she:
'I get it from you.'

Then he:
'Well, you don't take after her.
Not that I can see.'

He thinks of asking
about his bitter better half –
then thinks better of it.

* * * * *

Interior. Common Room.
Incontinent candles
squat in grease.
Ralph Clifford is telling Angelika
all about art. All about art:
that narrative, the best narrative,
flirts with the reader.
A flirtation that is sometimes a cock-tease.
Sometimes a tremendous fuck.

(He has drunk quite a lot.)

(Ainsworth, seeing himself outbid,
is silenced, sits with his eyes shut.
Injections of heartburn.)

'Life is trivial. Death is trivial.
None of this matters. Obviously.
Art is our pretence
that people are important.
It is our consolation.
Yes? Do you read me?'

Howard, Sir Alan, Charlie, Rasmus Petersen,
Ainsworth, Farley, Bennett, Pamela Johansson,
listen, unimportant, to his aria.

She can read him.

Attentive, shrewd Angelika
meditates on what the butler saw:
her eyed-up arse,
that automatic charm,
the reflex hints
of the habitually sexual,
his actual indifference.

'Once, religion soothed
our sense of insignificance.
The fall of a sparrow.
Nothing too negligible.
Lear expresses the opposite –
outrage at our unimportance.
"Why should a dog, a horse, a rat, have life,
And thou no breath at all?"
Our fucked-off friends may feel exploited
when they find they're in our books,
but what will survive of us,
and them, is art.'

Angelika the extra-muralist,
part-time at the CFE,
interrupts and amplifies:
'Like that Stoppard play,
when the playwright character,
Harry says (*The Real Thing*
just after the cricket bat bit)
that if you get the words right,
children will speak your poem for you
even though you're dead and gone.'

Awkward with high seriousness.
She has lost her reservations,
about herself, about Ralph Clifford,
faltered into confidence.
Ready to hit the high notes
in a well-read duet.
Her body a sound board:
one thickness spruce, special taper, sugar pine ribs…

Jealous Ainsworth, across the common room,
without opening his eyes:
'Then his wife, the actress, Annie,
recites what's written in his typewriter:
79. Interior. Commander's capsule.
He's working on a Sci-Fi film script.
Tommy Straussler, aka Stoppard,
downsizing the writer's ego.
Thank Christ. Not before time.
And it's Henry. Not Harry.'

Angelika silenced.
Academic Ainsworth cannot resist.
Even if, so up his own arse,
the know-all knows
he's kissing kissing Angelika's arse
goodbye for good.

The President addresses the ceiling:
'Dr Ainsworth's bedside manner,
my dear. His way of wooing.'

And to Ainsworth:
'Why not simply ask the girl
to clear up then clear out?'

And to Ralph Clifford:
'Ego sufficiently downsized?'

How to make an embryonic situation
explicit and impossible: thinks Howard.
Tactlessly rebuking the tactless.

Silence.

Sitting for a group portrait. So still.

More silence.

The President begins
to blow the candles out.
Small rococo smoke.
The acrid stink of ear-wax.

* * * * *

Bennett (Computer Sciences),
nude, up in the Old Tower,
is on his bare knees,
caressing his father's Mannlicher,
Angelika caught in the night sights.
She and the Butler
in aquarium light
laid back on the Harley-Davidson,
as it weaves, waddles,
to the college main gate.
Like Groucho Marx
he walks his Harley-Davidson.
As if it were a hobby-horse.

Bennett has asked her out. Twice.
And been refused, politely.
'My father forbids fraternisation
between staff and the SCR.'

(*Still harping on the daughter.*)

Bennett: of no importance.
And difficult to describe.
Nondescript nonentity. Dry skin.
Brittle, dusty hair,
strimmed rather than cut.
Brilliant, border-autistic,
when he talks
his head infinitesimally moves,
in synch to his lips.

Obsessed by Angelika.

Like everyone else.

When he comes,
in his head
he is holding her down.

Invisible.

Visible.

Acknowledgements: Pawel Pawlikowski suggested high table as the starting point for a film script – which turned into this poem. Thanks and apologies are due to him. Thanks also to my colleagues Will Poole and Michel Treisman who checked various 'facts'.

THE BRIDGE

Daniel Alarcón

Two days ago, at approximately 3.45 Thursday morning, a truck driver named Gregorio Rabassa misjudged the clearance beneath the pedestrian overpass on the thirty-second block of Avenida Cahuide. His truck, packed with washing machines and destined for a warehouse not far from there, hit the bottom of the bridge, shearing the top off his trailer and bringing part of the overpass down on to the avenue below. The back of the trailer opened on impact, spilling the appliances into the street. Fortunately, at the time of the accident there were no other cars on that stretch of road, and Mr Rabassa was not seriously injured. Emergency crews arrived within the hour, flooding Cahuide with light, and set about clearing the road of debris. Scraps of metal, pieces of concrete, the exploded insides of a few washing machines, all of it was loaded and carted away. Except for the ruined bridge, little evidence remained of the accident by the morning rush, and many people who lived nearby didn't even hear what had happened while they slept.

The neighbourhood to the east of Cahuide does not have one

name but many, depending on whom you ask. It is known most commonly as The Thousands, though many locals call it Venice, because of its tendency to flood. I've heard it referred to in news reports as Santa María, and indeed it does border that populous district, but the name is not exactly correct. A few summers ago, after a wave of kidnappings, police dotted the area with checkpoints and roadblocks, and the neighbourhood became known as Gaza, an odd, rather inexact reference to troubles on the other side of the world, only briefly and occasionally noted in the local press. How this nickname stuck is a mystery. The Thousands is an ordinary neighbourhood of working poor, crammed with modest brick houses lining narrow streets. It is set in the foggy basin between two hills and the only people who know it well are those who call it home. A turbid, slow-moving creek runs roughly parallel to Cahuide and is partially canalized, a project intended to alleviate the annual flooding but which has had, I am told, the opposite effect. The main road entering the neighbourhood is paved, as are most others, but some are not. My uncle Ramón, who was blind, lived there with his wife, Matilde, who was also blind, and their road, for instance, was not paved.

On Thursday morning, my uncle and his wife left their house early, as they always did, drank tea and chatted briefly with Señora Carlotta, who sells hot drinks and pastries from a cart at the corner of José Olaya and Avenida Unidad. She tells me they were in good spirits and that they held hands as they left, though she can't recall what it was they spoke about. 'Nothing really,' she said to me this afternoon when I went to visit. Her broad face and greying hair give the impression of someone who has seen a great deal from her perch at the corner of these two rather quiet neighbourhood streets. Her cheeks were wet and glistening as she spoke. 'We never talked about anything in particular,' she said, 'but I always looked forward to their visit. They seemed to be very much in love.'

Each working day, after drinking their tea and chatting with Carlotta, my blind uncle and his blind wife boarded the 73 bus to the city centre, a long meandering route that took over an hour, but

which left them within a few steps of their work. They were both employed as translators by a company whose offices are not far from the Judicial building where I work: Ramón specialized in English to Spanish; Matilde, Italian to Spanish. All sorts of people are willing to pay for the service and the work could be, from time to time, quite interesting. They would spend their days on the phone, transparent participants in bilingual conversations, translating back and forth between businessmen, government officials, or old couples in one country speaking to their grandchildren in another. Those cases are the most taxing, as the misunderstandings between two generations are far more complex than a simple matter of language.

I went to visit the offices yesterday in my lunch hour, to clean out their desks and talk to their colleagues. I have been named executor of their estate and these sorts of tasks are my responsibility now. Everyone had heard about the accident, of course, and seemed stunned by the news. I received condolences in eight languages from an array of dishevelled, poorly dressed men and women, who collectively gave the impression of hovering just slightly above what is commonly known as reality. Each translator wore an earpiece and a microphone, and seemed to have acquired, over the course of a career, or a lifetime, a greenish tint like that of the computer screen that sat before him. All around, the chatter was steady and oddly calming, like the sea, or an orchestra tuning up. One after another, the translators approached and shared a few hushed, accented words, all in a strange patois that seemed both related to and completely divorced from the local dialect. I had to strain to make out their words, and everything would end with an embrace, after which they would shuffle back to their desks, still lilting under their breath in a barely identifiable foreign language. Eventually, an elderly gentleman whose surname was Del Piero, who had worked in the Italian section with Matilde, pulled me aside and led me to a bank of ashy windows that looked out over a crowded side street. He was bent, had a thin, airy voice, and his breath smelled strongly of coffee. His sweater was old and worn, and looked as if you could pull a loose strand of yarn

and unravel the entire garment. Mercifully, he spoke a clear, only slightly accented Spanish. They had worked together for years. He thought of Matilde as his daughter, Del Piero told me, and he would miss her most of all. 'More than any of these other people,' he said, indicating the open floor of the translation offices with a disappointed nod. Did I hear him? He wanted to know if I could hear him.

'Yes,' I said. 'I hear you.'

'She was a saint, a miracle of a woman.'

I squeezed his arm and thanked him for his kind words. 'My uncle?' I asked.

'I knew him too.' Del Piero shrugged me off and straightened his sweater. 'We never got along,' he said. 'I don't speak English.'

I let this rather puzzling remark go by with barely a nod. We stared out the window for a moment, not speaking. A slow-moving line had formed along the wall on the street below, mostly elderly people, each clutching a piece of paper. Del Piero explained that on the last Friday of each month, one of the local newspapers held a raffle. Their offices were around the corner. You only had to turn in a completed crossword puzzle to enter. The man in a baseball cap leaning against the wall was, according to Del Piero, a dealer in completed crosswords. By his very stance, by the slouch of his shoulders, you might have guessed he was involved in something much more illicit – the trade in stolen copper, the trafficking of narcotics, the buying and selling of orphans. I had barely noticed him, but now it was clear: one after another the buyers approached, furtively slipped the man in the cap a coin or two, and took the paper he handed them. The old people rushed off with their answer key, to join the line and fill in the squares of their still incomplete puzzles.

'What are they giving away this month?'

'How should I know?' Del Piero said. 'Alarm clocks. Blenders. Washing machines like the ones that killed my Matilde.' His face went pallid. 'Your uncle wasn't blind. I know you won't believe me. But he murdered her, I just know he did.'

Del Piero muttered a few words to himself in Italian and then

walked back to his desk. I followed him. 'Explain yourself,' I said, but he shook his head sadly and slumped in his chair. He looked as if he might cry.

No one else seemed to notice our miniature drama and I wondered if translators in this office often fell to weeping in the course of their labours. I grabbed a chair and sat in front of his desk, staring at Del Piero as I do in court sometimes when I want a witness to know I will not relent. 'Say it again. Explain it to me.'

Del Piero raised a hand for a moment, then seemed to reconsider, letting it drop slowly to the desk. There were beads of sweat gathering at his temples. The man was wilting before me. 'What is there to explain? He could *see*. Your uncle moved around the office like a ballerina. I don't do anything all day, you know. No one speaks Italian any more. Two calls a day. Three at most. All from young men who want visas, boys whose great-grandfathers were born in Tuscany, or Palermo, or wherever. And I negotiate with a court clerk to get a copy of an ancient birth certificate. Do you realize that Italy barely existed as a nation then? All this fiction, all these elegant half-truths, just so yet another one of ours can flee! I know the score. They're all flying to Milan to get sex changes. Cheap balloon tits, like the girls in the magazines. Collagen implants. I can hear it in their voices. They're not cut out for life here. And so, what do I do? All day, I wait for the phone to ring, and while I wait, I watch them. The Chinese, the Arabs, the Hindus. I listen. I watch.'

'What are you talking about?'

'He could *see*, damn it. I know this. Matilde and I would sit by that window, waiting for the phone to ring, drinking coffee, and I would describe for her what was happening on the street below. That swarthy guy in the baseball cap – we talked about him every Friday! And she loved it. She said your uncle described things just as well. That he had a magical sense of direction, so perfect that at times she doubted he was blind.'

'He wasn't born like that, you know. What she said sounds like a compliment to me.'

'If you say so.' Del Piero looked unimpressed. 'They're going to fire me now.'

I didn't want to feel pity for him, but I couldn't help it.

He went on: 'Matilde would have quit in protest. She loved me that much. And if she quit, your uncle would have too. He was their best worker – they never would've let him walk. His English was better than the Queen's!'

The Queen? I stood to go. 'I appreciate your time,' I said, though his phone had been silent since I'd arrived.

Del Piero caught me looking. 'I got a call earlier. I might get another this afternoon.' Then he shrugged; he didn't believe it himself. He walked me out, his sad, heavy eyes trained at the floor. At the staircase, he stopped. *'Coloro che amiamo non ci abbandonano mai, essi vivono nei nostri ricordi,'* he said.

'Is that so?'

Del Piero nodded gravely. 'Indeed. It's not much, but it'll have to do.'

I thanked him. Whatever it meant, it did sound nice.

R amón lost his sight in a fireworks mishap at age seven, when I was only three. I have no memories of him before the accident, and to me he has always been my blind uncle. He was my father's youngest brother, half-brother actually, separated by more than twenty years, and you could say we grew up, if not together, then in parallel. By the time Ramón was born, my grandfather's politics had softened quite a bit, so the child was spared a Russian name. My grandfather lived with us, but I never heard him and my father exchange more than a few words. I spent my childhood ferrying messages between the two men – *Tell your father this, tell your grandfather that...* They'd had a falling out when I was very young, a political disagreement that morphed into a personal one, the details of which no one ever bothered to explain. Ramón's mother, my grandfather's last mistress, was a thin, delicate woman who never smiled, and when I was in elementary and middle school, she would

bring her boy over every week or so to see my grandfather. I was an only child in a funereal house and I liked the company. Ramón made a point of addressing me as *nephew*, and my father as *brother*, with such rigour that I understood his mother had taught him to do so. I didn't mind. He always had a new dirty joke to share, something beautifully vulgar he had learned from his classmates at the Normal School for Boys in the old city centre. He was a serious student of English even then, would record the BBC evening news on the short wave, and play it back, over and over, until he understood and could repeat every word. By then, the news might be two weeks old or more, but even so his dedication to the exercise always impressed me.

To my ear, the house got even quieter whenever Ramón and his mother arrived, but he liked our place for precisely the opposite reason: with its creaky wooden floors, he could hear himself coming and going, he said, and the space made sense to him. It was large and the high ceilings gave the human voice a sonority that reminded him of church. Sometimes he would ask me to lead him on a tour of the place, just to test his own impressions of the house, and we would shuttle up and down the steps, or tiptoe along the walls of the living room so he could trace its dimensions. He had memories of the house from before the accident, but they were dimmer each day, and he was aware that his brain had changed. It was changing still, he'd tell me ominously, even now, even at this very moment. I thought he was crazy, but I liked to hear him talk. My mother had lined the stairwell with framed photographs, and Ramón would have me describe what seemed to be quite ordinary family scenes of birthday parties and vacations, my school pictures, or my father with a client celebrating some legal victory.

'Am I in any of them?' Ramón asked me once, and the question caught me so off guard that I said nothing. I remember a ball of pain in the hollow of my stomach and panic spreading slowly up to my chest, my arms. I held my breath until Ramón began laughing.

He would have been forty-four this year.

The centrepiece of each visit was a closed-door sit-down with my

grandfather. They spoke about Ramón's studies, his plans, my ailing grandfather dispensing stern bits of wisdom gathered from his forty years as a municipal judge. I was always a bit jealous of these; the undivided attention my grandfather gave Ramón was something my father never gave me. But by the time I was ten, the old man was barely there, his moments of lucidity increasingly brief, until everything was a jumble of names and dates, and he could barely recognize any of us. In the twenty-odd years since my grandfather passed away, my father's mind has collapsed in a similar, if slightly more erratic pattern, as perhaps mine will too, eventually. My inheritance, such as it is.

One day, after Ramón's conversation with my grandfather, he and I went on a walk through the neighbourhood. I must have been twelve or thirteen. We were only a few blocks from my house when Ramón announced that he wouldn't be coming to visit any more. 'There's no point,' he said. He was finishing school and would soon be attending the university on a scholarship. We were walking in the sun, along the wide, tree-lined median that ran down the main avenue of my district. Ramón, with a hand in his pocket, had insisted on going barefoot so he could feel the texture of the grass between his toes. He had tied the laces of his sneakers and wore them slung around his neck.

'What about me?' I said.

He smiled at the question. 'You're a lucky boy. You live with your dad.'

I had nothing to say to that.

'Do you want to see something?' Ramón took his hand from his pocket, opening it to reveal a small spool of copper wire, bent and coiled into an impossible knot. I asked him what it was.

'It's a map,' he said.

I took it when he passed it to me, careful not to disturb its shape.

'Every time we turn, I bend it,' he explained. 'And so I never get lost.'

'Never?'

'I'm very careful with it.'

'It's nice,' I said, because that was all I could think to say.

Ramón nodded. 'My father isn't coming back. Your grandfather. His mind has…' He cupped his hands together, then opened them with a small sound, as if he'd been holding a tiny bomb that had just gone off.

'The old guy's not going to miss me.'

The sun was bright and Ramón turned toward it, so that his face glowed. I couldn't deny that he looked very happy.

When we got back to the house, my grandfather was in the living room, asleep in front of the television, taking shallow breaths through his open mouth. He'd been watching opera and now Ramón's mother sat by his side, combing his hair. She stood when she saw her son, nodding at me without a hint of warmth, and then gathered her things. She left the comb balanced on my grandfather's knee.

'It's time to go,' she said. 'Careful. Don't wake your father. Now say goodbye to your nephew.'

He shook my hand very formally, and I saw little of him after that.

My grandfather died two years later.

L ast night, I couldn't sleep. For hours, I lay on my back, the bedside lamp on, admiring the ceiling and its eerie yellow tint. My wife slept with the blanket pulled over her head, so still it was possible to imagine I was all alone. I thought of the truck, out of control and speeding, tearing the bridge down as it raced south. Or Ramón, walking Matilde steadily, lovingly, to her death. In their haste, the local emergency crews neglected to block off the bridge's stairs on either side of the avenue. Four hours later, my uncle and aunt climbed these same stairs on their way to the bus stop, but they never made it, of course, tumbling on to the avenue instead, where they were killed by oncoming traffic. It had been in all the afternoon papers on Thursday, along with photos of the truck driver, Rabassa, an unshaven young man with a sheepish smile, who wore his light brown hair in a ponytail. In interviews, he offered his heartfelt

condolences to the families, but, on the advice of counsel, had little else to say about the accident. I would have given him the same advice. In the classic understated style common to our local journalists, the ruined bridge was now being called THE BRIDGE OF DEATH, or alternatively THE BRIDGE TO DEATH. At home, my wife and I instructed the maid to let the phone ring, and at the office, I asked my secretary to screen all the calls and hang up on radio, television or print reporters. It was only a matter of time, and by yesterday morning, when it was discovered that Ramón was related to my father, the scrutiny intensified. There were now two scandals in play. In the afternoon, when I went to pick my daughters up from school, a young reporter, a boy of no more than twenty, followed me to my car, asking for a comment, for anything, a phrase, a string of expletives, a word, a cry of pain. He had hungry eyes and the sort of untrustworthy smile common to youth here: he could commit neither to smiling nor to frowning, the thin edges of his lips suspended somewhere in between. 'Do you plan to sue?' he shouted, as my daughters and I hurried toward the car.

Last night I read the afternoon editions very carefully, with something approximating terror: what if someone had managed to get through to my father, to prise a comment from him? It would be difficult, given his situation, but not unthinkable, and surely he would oblige with something outrageous, something terrible. I bought a dozen papers and read every page – testimonials from neighbours, interviews with civil engineers and trucking experts, comments from the outraged president of a community advocacy group and the reticent spokesman of the transport workers' union, along with photos of the site – a hundred opinions through which to filter this ordinary tragedy, but thankfully nothing from my father, and not on the television either.

This morning, Saturday, I went to see my old man to tell him the news myself and make certain the asylum's authorities were aware that soon the press would be calling. Apparently there had been attempts already, but I was relieved to discover my father had lost

more of his privileges, including just last week the right to receive incoming calls. He'd long ago been barred from making them. Of course, there were some cellphones floating among the population of the asylum, so the secretary couldn't offer me any guarantees. She didn't know all the details, but his nurse, she assured me, would explain everything.

My old man has been in the asylum for three years now. He is only sixty-eight, young to be in the shape he's in. Every time I go, he's different, as if he's trying on various pathologies to see how they suit him. It happened so slowly I hardly noticed, until the day three and a half years ago that he attacked a man in court – his own client – stabbing him multiple times in the neck and chest with a letter opener, nearly killing him. It came as a great surprise to us, and the press loved the story. It went on for months, and no aspect of the scandal went unreported. For example, it was noted with evident delight that my father's client, the victim – on trial for money laundering – might serve time with his former lawyer if convicted. One columnist used the matter to discuss the possibility of prison reform, while a rather mean-spirited political cartoonist presented the pair as lovers, holding hands and playing house in a well-appointed prison cell. My mother stopped answering the phone or reading the papers; in fact, she rarely left home. But none of this chatter was relevant in the end: the money launderer was acquitted; my father was not.

His trial was mercifully brief. My old man, charged with assault and attempted murder, facing a prison sentence that would take him deep into his eighties, wisely opted for an insanity plea. Out of respect for his class and professional history, room was made for him at the asylum, and though it was jarring at first, over time he has become essentially indistinguishable from the other guests.

I was shown to the visitors' room by a pale, tired-looking nurse who told me my old man had been in a bad mood recently. 'He's been acting out.'

I'd never seen her before. 'Are you new?' I asked.

She walked briskly and I struggled to keep up. She told me she'd been transferred from the women's pavilion. I tried to make small talk, about how things were over there, if she was adjusting to the inevitable differences between the genders, but she wasn't interested and only wanted to tell me about my father. 'He's a real sweetheart,' she said, and she was worried about him. He wasn't eating and some days he refused to take his medication. The previous week, he had tossed his plate at a man who happened to bump him in the lunch line. 'It was spaghetti day. You can imagine the mess.'

In case I couldn't, she went on to describe it: how my old man walked calmly from his victim, sat in front of a television in a corner of the cafeteria watching a nature show with the sound off, waiting for the nurses to arrive; how when they did, he crossed his wrists and held his arms out in front of him, as if expecting handcuffs, which, she assured me, 'we rarely use with men like your father'. Meanwhile, a few terrified patients had begun to cry: they thought the victim was bleeding to death before their very eyes, that those were his organs spilling from his wounded body. The nurse sighed heavily. All sorts of ideas held sway among the residents of the asylum. Some believed in thieves who stole men's kidneys, their livers and their lungs, and it was impossible to convince them otherwise.

We had come to a locked door. I thanked her for telling me.

'You should visit him more often,' she said.

A fluorescent light shone above us, cold, clinical. I kept my gaze fixed on her, until I could see the colour gathering in her cheeks. I straightened my tie.

'Should I?' I said. 'Is that what you think?'

The nurse looked down at her feet, suddenly fidgety and nervous. 'I'm sorry.' She pulled a keyring from her jacket pocket and, as she did, her silver cigarette case fell with a crash, a dozen long, thin smokes fanning out across the cement floor like the confused outline of a corpse.

I bent to help her gather them. Her face was very red now.

'My name is Yvette,' she said. 'If you need anything.'

I didn't answer.

Then we were through the door and into a large, rather desolate common room. There were a few ragged couches and a pressboard bookcase along a white wall, its shelves picked almost clean, save for a thin volume on canoe repair, a yellowing cold war spy novel and some fashion magazines with half the pages missing. There were a dozen men, not more, and the room was quiet.

Where was everyone?

Yvette explained that many of the patients – she had used this word all along, not inmates, or prisoners as some others did – were still in the cafeteria and some had retired to their rooms.

'Cells?' I asked.

Yvette pursed her lips. 'If you prefer.' She continued: many were outside, in the gardens. The morning had dawned clear in this part of the city and I imagined a careless game of volleyball, a couple of men standing flat-footed on either side of a sagging net, and quickly realized these were images culled from movies, that in fact I had no idea how those confined against their will to a hospital for the criminally insane might make use of a rare day of bright, limpid sun. They might lie in the grass and nap, or pick flowers, listen for birds or the not-so-distant sounds of city traffic. Or perhaps glide across the open yard, its yellow grass ceding territory each day to the bare, dark earth, these so-called gardens, each inmate just one man within a ballet much larger, much lonelier than himself. My father preferred to stay indoors. Early on he wasn't permitted outside and so had become, like a house cat, accustomed to watching from the windows, too proud to admit any interest in going out himself. In the three years I've been visiting him, we'd walked the gardens only once: one grey morning beneath a solemn sky, on his birthday, his first after the divorce. He'd walked with his head down the entire time. I mentioned this and Yvette nodded.

'Well, they're not exactly gardens, you know.'

Just as Yvette was not exactly a nurse, this prison was not exactly a hospital. Of course I knew. I watched a woman read to a group of

inmates, what amounted to a children's story, and she could hardly get through a sentence without being interrupted. My father sat in his usual spot, by the high window in the far corner, overlooking a few little-used footpaths that wended between the trees surrounding the main building. He was alone, which upset me, until I noticed that all the patients in this group were essentially alone; even the ones who were, nominally at least, together. A dozen solitary men scattered about, lost in thought or drugged into somnolence, in a room in which eye contact, the very bedrock of human interaction, seemed to be frowned upon.

Yvette brushed my arm and excused herself wordlessly.

I made my way toward my father, past a small table along a salmon-coloured wall, stacked with games and pamphlets, and a bulletin board just above it, announcing the week's programme – POETRY NIGHT, SPORTS NIGHT, CEVICHE NIGHT. Hardly an evening passed, as far as I could tell, without a planned activity of some kind; it was no wonder these men seemed so tired. They all wore their own clothes, ranging from the shabby to the somewhat elegant, and this lack of uniform dress operated as a kind of shorthand, revealing at first glance which of these men had been abandoned and which still maintained, however tenuously, some connection to the world outside. There were dishevelled men in threadbare, faded T-shirts and others who looked as if they might have a business meeting later, who still took the trouble to keep their leather shoes oiled and polished. A man in denim overalls sat at one of the two long tables writing a letter. An unplugged television was placed at an angle to the small couch, its grey, bulbous eye reflecting the light pouring in through the windows. The curtains were pulled, but the windows themselves did not open, and the room was quite warm.

I sat on the windowsill.

'Hi, Papa,' I said.

He didn't respond, only closed his eyes, gripping the arms of his chair as if to steady himself. He looked like my grandfather had so many years ago, shrunken, with long, narrow fingers, the bones of

his hands visible beneath the skin. I hadn't seen him in six weeks or so. I asked him how he was, and he looked up and all around me, gazing above me and beyond me, with a theatrical expression of utter confusion, as if he were hearing a voice and couldn't figure where it was coming from.

'Me?' he asked. 'Little old me?'

I waited.

'I'm fine,' my father said. 'A robust specimen of old age in the twilight of Western civilization. It's not me you should worry about. Someone snuck a newspaper in here two weeks ago. You can't imagine the scandal it caused. Is it true the oceans are rising?'

'I suppose so,' I said.

He sighed. 'When will the Americans learn? I can picture it – can you picture it? The seas on a slow boil, turning yellow, turning red. The fish rise to the surface. They feel pain, you know. Those people who say they don't are liars.'

'Who says that?'

'Water heightens sensitivity, boy. When I was a child, I loved to sit in the bathtub. I liked watching my cock float in the bathwater and then shrivel and shrink as the water got cold.'

'Papa.'

'Sometimes it's so loud in here, I can't breathe. I will break that television if anyone attempts to turn it on. I will pick it up and break it over the head of anyone who goes near it. Just keep your eye on it. Just tell me if someone plugs it in. Will you do that, boy?'

I nodded, if only to keep him calm, and tried to imagine the act. My father versus the television: his back would crumble, his fingers crack, what remained of his body would collapse into a thimbleful of dust. The television would emerge unscathed; my father most certainly would not. When he spoke he waved his arms, fidgeted and shook, and even these small gestures seemed to be wearing him out. He was breathing heavily, his bird chest rising and falling.

'The nurse says you haven't been eating.'

'The menu is not interesting,' my old man said. He bit his

bottom lip.

'And your meds? Are they interesting?'

He glared at me for a second. 'Honestly, no. There is a gentleman here with whom I have made a small wager. He says there is a women's pavilion, not far from this building, loose women, crazier than hell. They tear your clothes off with their teeth. I say that's impossible. What do you know of it?'

'It's a beautiful day, Papa. We could go out and see for ourselves.'

'No need for that.'

'What does the winner of this wager get?'

My father smiled. 'Money, boy – what else?'

'I don't know anything about it, Papa,' I said, 'but I have some news.'

At the sound of these words, after all the talk and movement, he fixed his stare on me, nodding, then closed his eyes to indicate he was listening.

'Ramón. Your brother Ramón. He's dead.'

My father squinted at me. 'The young one?'

I nodded. 'Has anyone called you about this?'

He looked surprised. 'Called me? Why would anyone call me?'

'The press, I mean. Have you talked to anyone?'

He dismissed the very idea with a wave of his hand. 'Of course not,' he said. 'Am I in the papers?'

'The usual.'

He smiled with a melancholy pride. 'They don't get tired of me.'

'I'm executor of the estate,' I said.

'What estate? Ramón doesn't have an estate!' My old man laughed. 'Let me guess... You're *honoured*.'

I could have hit him then. It happens every time I visit, and each time I breathe, I wait for it to pass. And I think of my daughters, who will never see their grandfather again, and specifically of my youngest, who has no memories of him at all.

'How did it happen?' my old man asked.

And so I told him the story, what I knew of it – Rabassa's truck

and the washing machines, the pedestrian bridge and the bus – as my father listened with eyes closed, letting his chin drop to his chest. As I recounted the events, the order of them, their inevitable conclusion, it sounded so asinine I felt he might not believe me at all. They had not been close. They had spoken little since my grandfather died, after the unpleasant work of dividing up the inheritance had been rendered to our advantage with the help of a small platoon of lawyers and consultants. Ramón used his share to support his mother and, when she passed away, to buy the house where he and Matilde lived. There was little left over for anything else. My father's sister, my aunt Natalya, and his full brother, my uncle Yuri, pooled their shares and bought a condo in Miami overlooking Biscayne Bay. My father got the bulk of the estate, of course, enough to live comfortably for many years, and eventually to cover his defence, the divorce settlement, his upkeep at the asylum. He even set aside a portion for me, his only child, which my wife and I used as a down payment on a house in a part of the city with only one name and no pedestrian bridges. We have lived there since we were married eight years ago.

When I finished, he was quiet for a long moment and seemed to be processing what I had told him. He could have just as easily been trying to recall who this brother was, and why it should bother him that Ramón was dead.

'She wasn't blind,' my father said finally. 'That bitch had cataracts, it's true, but she could see. She killed him.'

For a moment, I couldn't say anything; I just stared at my father, wondering why I'd bothered. 'Jesus,' I said. 'She sure seemed blind at the wedding.'

My father looked at me. 'How do you *seem* blind?'

'I was joking.'

'Jokes,' he said, disgusted. 'I don't like your jokes.' He stood abruptly. His shirt hung off him like a robe and his belt had been pulled tight to the last hole, cinching his pants high above his waist, the fabric ballooning about his midsection. I reached to help him, but he shook me off.

'Papa, you have to eat,' I said.

He ignored me, covered his eyes with one hand and began walking slowly, with heavy, plodding steps, staggering toward the centre of the room, a shaky arm raised before him. He stumbled toward the lesser of the two couches, where a nicely dressed gentleman sat thumbing through a pornographic comic book. As my father approached, the man cried out and fled. I called out to my father, but he paid no attention, only changed direction, moving toward one of the tables now. There, the man writing the letter abandoned his work and shuffled off to the corner of the room. The nurse who had been reading saw what was happening, tucked her black hair behind her ears and hurried over to find out what was the matter, but I got to my father first, this blind, wobbling zombie; I put an arm around him, holding him gently, his thin frame, his hollow chest.

It took almost no effort to restrain him.

'I'm blind, I'm blind,' he murmured.

I listened to the cadence of his breath. The other inmates had spread out to the pink corners of the room, as far as they could manage from my old man. They eyed one another tensely and no one spoke. Just then, the black-haired nurse appeared before us. She wanted to know if everything was all right.

'Yes,' I said, but my father shook his head. He cleared his throat, and it was only then that he dropped his hand from over his eyes, blinking as he adjusted to the light.

'Alma,' he said, 'my brother has died and I am bereft. I must be released for the funeral. He has been murdered. It is a tragedy.'

The nurse looked at my old man, then at me. I shook my head very slightly, hoping he wouldn't notice.

'Mr Cano, I'm very sorry for your loss.' Alma sounded as if she were reading from a script.

Still my father thanked her. 'You're very kind, but I must leave at once. There are details to be taken care of.'

'I'm afraid that's not possible.'

'My brother…'

'Papa,' I said.

'Mr Cano, you cannot leave without a judge's approval.'

I held my father and felt the strength gather within him at the very sound of these words. He puffed up, his shoulders straightened. This was likely the least effective pretext one could give my father, the son of a judge, a man who had spent first his childhood and then his entire adult life wandering the corridors of judicial power, a man who had passed on to his own son, if little affection, at least much of this same access. He smiled triumphantly and turned to me. 'Your cellphone, please, boy. I know a few judges.'

I pretended to search my pockets for my phone, as my old man watched me hopefully. By then Yvette had joined us, somehow gentler than I had noticed her to be at first, and she met his gaze, then touched his shoulder, and just like that he slipped from my hold and into her orbit entirely.

'They've murdered my brother…' I heard my old man say, his voice mournful and low. Yvette nodded, leading him to the blue-green couch, and he went without a fight, collapsing into it heavily. She kneeled next to him. Alma went off to soothe the other patients, who had been watching us with great anxiety, and suddenly I was alone. I could hear Yvette and my father murmuring conspiratorially, fraternally, now laughing tenderly, a voice breaking, now humming in unison what sounded like a nursery rhyme. With Alma's encouragement, the other inmates were gradually spreading about the room again, in slow, tentative steps, as if trying to move without being seen. Yvette walked over to me.

'I'm sorry about your uncle,' she said.

She glanced back at my father and then left us alone. I took her spot beside him and together we watched the men drifting back to their former places. The days here, I realized, were punctuated by these outbursts, these small crises that help break up the hours. These men had been socialized to expect discrete moments of tension, to defer to the impulse, whether theirs or someone else's, to fashion a

disturbance from thin air. And they were experts, too, at forgetting it all, at recovering, at turning back into themselves and whatever private despair kept them company. Except one of them: a slight, well-dressed man pacing back and forth in front of me and my father, occasionally pausing to flash us a confused glare. It took me a moment to realize what had happened: he carried a comic book in his right hand. We'd taken his seat.

I pointed him out to my father and he shrugged. 'I've never seen him before in my life.'

'He was sitting right here.'

'Of course. They were all sitting right here. And they can all sit right here again as soon as I get up.'

'Papa, don't get upset.'

'I'm not upset,' he said, then corrected himself. 'That's not true. I *am* upset. I would prefer he stop staring. It's rude. Tonight I will take his belt and hang him with it.'

I sighed. 'Why would you do that, Papa?'

'I don't know,' he said, his voice suddenly weak.

It was honest at least: he *didn't* know. My father remained, all these years later, the person most mystified by his predicament, by the actions and impulses that had brought him here. 'It's okay, Papa.' I tried to put an arm around him, but he shook me off.

'It's not okay. I'm going to die here. Not tomorrow, not next week, but eventually. The oceans are rising and my blind brother has been murdered. My ungrateful son never visits and my whore-wife has forgotten me.'

'Ex-wife,' I said. I didn't mean to.

My father scowled, his gaze narrowing. 'Whore-ex-wife,' he said. 'Go. No one wants you here. Leave.'

The last time I saw Ramón was at a family party, about three years ago. It was my father's sixty-fifth birthday, his first since the arrest. This was before the divorce got under way and my mother was still hanging in there. We decided to get my old man out for the

party, just for the evening – not an easy task, but certainly not unheard of for a family of our connections and our means. I was optimistic in the weeks before the party, and saw to it that my mother was as well. I thought it would be good for them both, to see each other, and especially good for him to be reminded of the life he'd once had. I paid courtesy visits to bureaucrats all over town, spoke elliptically about my father's situation and looked for the right opening, the right moment, to place money discreetly in the hands of those men who might be able to help us. But nothing happened: my calls went unreturned, the openings were never provided. In the end, I had to tell my mother, only hours before the party, that the director of the asylum, whom I had spoken to directly and pressured through various surrogates, wouldn't take the bribe, just as no judge would sign the order and no prison official would allow themselves to be bent. My father wouldn't be joining us.

She had spent a lifetime with him and become accustomed to getting her way. It was clear she didn't believe me. 'How much did you offer?'

'More than enough,' I told her. 'No one wants to help him any more.'

My mother sat before her mirror, delicately applying make-up, her reddish-brown hair still pulled back. She had outlined her lips and examined them now, getting so close to the glass I thought she might kiss herself. 'It's not that. It's not that at all,' she said. 'You just didn't try hard enough.'

That night Ramón arrived by himself, dressed as if for a funeral in a sober black suit and starched white shirt. His hair was cut so short that he looked like an enlisted man, or a police officer, and he had chosen to come without the dark glasses he sometimes wore. I'd never seen him this way. I was surprised to find him there, as was my mother, and for a moment much of the whispered conversation at the party had to do with his presence: who had invited Ramón? How did he know? Why had he come? I led him through the thin crowd of friends and well-wishers, introducing him to everyone. *Oh, you're*

Vladimiro's younger brother, some colleague of my father's might say, though for most of them, this was the first they'd ever heard of Ramón. If he noticed the chatter, he didn't let on. There were many fewer guests than we had imagined – even my uncle Yuri had called with an excuse – and the brightly decorated room seemed rather dismal with only a handful of people milling around. It was early yet, I told myself. Ramón moved easily through the party, falling gracefully in and out of various conversations. He let go of my arm every time we stopped before a new group of people, holding his hand out and waiting for someone to shake it. Eventually, someone would. He held Natalya in a long embrace, whispering, *Dear sister, dear dear sister*. I left him chatting with my wife while I went for drinks, and our daughters, three and four years old at the time, climbed into his arms without hesitation. He beamed for a quick photo, and then released them, and measured their height against his waist. My wife told me later that he had remembered not only their names, but also their birthdays and their ages, though he hadn't seen them since my youngest was born.

My mother had positioned herself at the landing of the staircase, at one end of the large room, where she could survey the entire affair, and eventually we made our way over to her. Ramón asked me to leave them alone. They huddled together for a few moments, whispering, and when my mother raised her head again, her eyes were glassy with tears. She gathered herself and called for everyone's attention. Ramón stood by her side. She began by thanking everyone for coming to celebrate this difficult birthday, how much it meant to all of us, to my father and his family. 'We did what we could to have him here with us this evening, but it just wasn't possible,' she said. She looked at me. 'My husband has sent his youngest brother Ramón in his place and I want to thank him for coming to be with us.'

After acknowledging the polite applause, Ramón scanned the crowd, or seemed to, his lifeless grey eyes flitting left and right. There couldn't have been more than fifteen people altogether, everyone standing, waiting for something to happen. Someone coughed.

Ramón asked that the music be turned down, cleared his throat, then went on to describe a version of my father I didn't recognize. A generous man, always available with a loving hand for his younger brother, a man who had helped guide and encourage him. Who had sat with him 'after the accident that left me blind, the accident that made me who I am'. My mother was sobbing softly now. 'Vladimiro helped pay for my studies. He paid for my tutor and helped me land the job where, by the grace of God, I was to meet my wife, Matilde.' Then he raised a hand and began singing 'Happy Birthday', his voice clear and unwavering.

He sang the first line entirely alone before anyone thought to join in.

I found him, not long after, sitting in what had been my grandfather's favourite chair. He smiled when he heard my voice, he called me *nephew*. I asked him about life. It had been so long since we'd really talked. Matilde was well, he told me, they'd bought a house in The Thousands – *Where?* I thought to myself – and were talking about having a baby. He congratulated me on my family and said, with a playful smile, that he could tell by the timbre of my wife's voice that she was still quite beautiful. I laughed at the compliment.

'Your instincts are, as ever, unfailing,' I said.

We were – my wife and I – very happy in those days.

Ramón talked briefly about his work, which in spite of the feeble economy remained steady: Italian was an increasingly irrelevant language, of course, but as long as America remained powerful, he and Matilde would never go hungry. Each day he took calls from the Embassy, the DEA or the Mormons. They trusted him. They asked for him by name.

We fell silent. The party hummed around us and, looking at our uncomfortable guests, I wondered why anyone would want to be part of our family.

'How did my father sound,' I asked, 'when you talked to him?'

Ramón ran his fingernails along the fabric of armrest. 'I didn't actually speak to him, you know. He had someone call me.'

He paused and let out a small, sharp laugh. 'I haven't spoken to him in years, to be honest. Not since Matilde and I were married. I guess he couldn't get to a phone. I assume they're very strict about those things.'

'I guess so.'

'But then, I've heard you can get anything in prison,' he said. 'Is that true?'

'It's not exactly a prison, where he is.'

'But he could've called me himself if he'd wanted to?'

I looked over my shoulder at the thinning party. 'He's never called me, if that's what you want to know.'

Ramón tapped his fingers to the slow rhythm of the music that was playing, an old bolero, something my father would've liked.

'That was quite a performance,' I said. 'Your speech, I mean.'

'It was for your mother.'

'Then I suppose I should thank you.'

'If you like.' He sighed. 'My father loved Vladimiro very much. He was so proud of your dad, he talked about him all the time. He was heartbroken that they'd stopped speaking.'

'Is that true?'

'Why do you ask if you won't believe my answer?' Ramón shook his head. 'Do you visit him?'

'As much as I can.'

'What's that mean?'

'As much as I can stand to.'

Ramón nodded. 'He's not an easy man. Matilde didn't want me to come. She has a sense about these things. And she's never wrong.'

I thought he might explain this comment, but he didn't. It just lingered. 'So why are you here?' I asked.

'Family is family.' He smiled. 'That's what I told her. She had quite a laugh with that one.'

And then, this afternoon, I went to Gaza. I took the bus, because I wanted to ride the 73 and sit, as Ramón and Matilde so often had, in

the uncomfortable metal seats, beside the scratched and dirty windows, closing my eyes and listening to the breathing city as it passed. The air thickened as we rode south, so that it felt almost like rain, heavy, grey and damp. The further we went on Cahuide, the slower the traffic became, and when I got off at the thirty-second block, beneath the remains of the bridge, I saw why: a stream of people filtered across the avenue in a nearly unbroken line, women carrying babies, stocky young men bent beneath the loads teetering on their backs, and children who appeared to be scampering across just for the sport of it. The median fence was no match for this human wave: already it had been knocked over, trampled, and appeared in places to be in danger of disappearing entirely. The harsh sounds of a dozen horns filled the street with an endless noise that most people seemed not to notice, but which shook my skull from the inside. I stopped for a moment to admire the bridge, its crumbling green exterior and shorn middle, its steel rods poking through the concrete and bending down toward the avenue. A couple of kids sat at the scarred edge, their legs dangling just over the lip. They laughed and floated paper airplanes into the sky, arcing them elegantly above the rushing crowd.

I walked up from the avenue along an unnamed street no wider than an alley, blocked off at one end with stacks of bricks and two rusting oil drums filled with sand. A rope hung limply between the drums and I slipped under it, careful not to let it touch my suit. A boy on a bicycle rolled by, smacking his chewing gum loudly as he passed. He did a loop around me, staring, sizing me up, then pedalled off, unimpressed. I kept walking to where the road sloped up just slightly, widening into a small outdoor market, where a few people milled about the stalls stocked with plastics and off-brand clothes and flowers and grains.

I came to the corner of José Olaya and Avenida Unidad, and there I found Carlotta. The lawyer who'd called me yesterday with the news had advised me to look for a woman at a tea cart. She can show you the house, he said over the phone. Your house. That afternoon,

as promised, a courier came by with Ramón's keys, along with a handwritten note from the lawyer once again reiterating this small piece of advice: look for Carlotta, the note read, though there was no description of her. You'll never find the house without help.

In fact, it did all look the same, each street indistinguishable from the last, each house a version of the one next to it. Carlotta was sitting on a small wooden stool reading a newspaper when I walked up. I introduced myself and explained that I needed to take a look at my uncle's house. She stood very slowly and wrapped me in a tight embrace.

'They were so wonderful,' she said. She kept her hand on mine and didn't let go, just stood there, shaking her head and murmuring what sounded like a prayer. I waited for her to finish. Finally she excused herself, went inside the unpainted brick house just behind her and emerged a few moments later dragging a boy along. He was eighteen or so, skinny, and looked as if he'd just been sleeping. He wore unlaced white high-top sneakers with no socks and his thin, almost girlish ankles emerged from these clownish shoes with a comic poignancy. Her son, Carlotta explained, would watch the stand while we went to Ramón and Matilde's house. It wasn't far. The boy glanced in my direction through red, swollen eyes, then nodded, though he seemed displeased with the arrangement.

As Carlotta and I walked up the street, she pointed out a few neighbourhood landmarks: the first pharmacy in the area, the first Internet kiosk, an adobe wall pockmarked with bullet holes, site of a murder that had made the news a few years ago. A police checkpoint, from the days when the name Gaza came into use, had stood right at the intersection we strolled through now. These were peaceful times, she said. She showed me the footbridge that crossed over the canal, and the open field just beyond it, where the turbid flood waters gathered once a year or so. It was where the teenagers organized soccer tournaments, where the Christians held their monthly revivals and where a few local deejays threw parties that lasted until first light. Awful music, she said, like a blast furnace, just noise. Her son had

DANIEL ALARCÓN

been at one of those, she told me, just last night. He was her youngest
boy. 'He's not a bad kid. I don't want you thinking he's trouble. Do
you have children?'

'Two daughters.'

She sighed. 'But girls are different.'

We turned left just before the footbridge and walked a way along
the canal, then turned left again to the middle of the block, stopping
in front of a saffron-yellow house. It was the only one painted on the
entire street.

'It's yellow,' I said to Carlotta, disbelieving. 'Why is it yellow?'

She shrugged. 'He did translations, favours. People paid him
however they could.'

'By painting a blind man's house?'

Carlotta didn't seem to find it that funny, or remarkable at all. 'We
called your uncle *Doctor*,' she said, and gave me a stern look. 'Out
of respect.'

I said nothing. There was a metal gate over the door, two
deadbolts, and it took a moment to find the right keys. I'd never been
to their house before and I felt suddenly guilty visiting for the first
time under these circumstances. Just inside the door there were a
jacket and hat hanging from a nail, and below it, a small, two-tiered
shoe rack containing rubber mud boots, beige men's and women's
slippers and two pairs of matching Velcro sneakers. There were a
couple of empty spaces on the rack. For their work shoes, I supposed,
the ones they had died in. Without saying a word, Carlotta and I left
our shoes behind and walked on into the house, wearing only our
socks. We didn't take the slippers.

The space was neatly laid out, as I had assumed it would be, and
dark, with no light bulbs anywhere and no photos, not of family, not
of each other. Because the long, damp winters are even longer and
damper in this part of the city, heavy translucent plastic sheeting
hung from every door jamb in wide strips, so that moving from one
room to another required a motion not unlike swimming the
butterfly stroke. The idea was to trap heat in each room, but the

effect, along with the hazy light, was to give the house the look and feel of an aquarium. I parted the plastic curtains and found myself in a sparsely furnished kitchen, kept in meticulous order. The refrigerator was nearly empty and there were no extra utensils in the drawers, just a pair of everything – two forks, two spoons, two steak knives. I opened the tap and a thin line of water dribbled into a single dirty bowl. There was another one, a clean bowl already dry, sitting by the sink.

I walked to the bedroom, as spare and clean as the kitchen, where a small wooden cross hung just above the neatly made bed. I opened and closed a few drawers, looked into the closet, and found two pairs of glasses in a box on top of the dresser, one with plastic yellow lenses, one with blue. I tried on the yellow pair, charmed by this small evidence of my uncle's vanity, and even found myself looking for a mirror. Of course, there wasn't one. This is all mine, I thought, to dispose of as I see fit. To sell, or rent, or burn, or give away. There was nothing of my family in this house and maybe that was the only attractive thing about it. My father kept everything of any value and Ramón got everything else, all this nothing – these clothes, this cheap furniture, this undecorated room and nondescript house, this parcel of land in a neighbourhood whose name no one could agree on. It was all paid for, the lawyer told me, they owned it outright, and my uncle had no debts to speak of. Unfortunately, he also had no heirs besides his wife, and she had none besides him. I was the nearest living relative.

After a long pause, the lawyer added: 'Well, except for your father.'

'What do I do with it?'

'See if there's anything you want to keep. You can sell the rest. It's up to you.'

And now I was here, hidden in The Thousands. At home, my phone was ringing, the city's frantic journalists demanding a statement. Soon they would be camping out in front of the asylum, tossing handwritten notes over the walls and into the gardens, or

crowding before the door to my house, harassing my children, my wife. Say something, entertain us with your worries, your fears, your discontent, blame your father, the men who built the bridge, or the ponytailed truck driver. Blame your blind uncle, his blind wife, the fireworks vendors, or yourself. My head hurt. I miss Ramón, I thought, and just as quickly the very idea seemed selfish. I hadn't seen him in years.

Carlotta had stayed in the living room and from the hallway I watched her blurred outline through the plastic. I swam through the house to see her.

'Are you all right?' I asked. 'I'm sorry to make you wait.'

She had nested into the soft cushions of my uncle and aunt's white sofa. There was a throw rug on the floor, somewhere near the middle of the room, and the soles of her feet hung just above, not touching it. Her hands lay in her lap. She seemed much younger in the subdued light of my uncle's home, her skin glowing, and her hair, greying in the daylight, appeared, in this shadowed room, to be almost black.

'What are you looking for?' she asked.

It was a fair question for which I had no answer.

'Nothing,' I said. 'Maybe I could live here.'

Carlotta smiled generously. 'You're not feeling well,' she said.

My wife would be surprised this evening when I told her about my day. She listened patiently as we prepared the meal, our daughters clamouring for our attention, and told me only that I must be careful. That places like that weren't safe. She'd never been to The Thousands or Venice or Gaza but, like all of us, believed many things about our city without needing them confirmed. Hadn't there been a famous murder there a few years ago? And didn't this latest accident only prove again that our world had nothing to do with that one? And I agreed quietly, yes, dear, you're right, he was my uncle, my brother, but I barely knew him – and I stopped my story there. I walked around the counter, gave her a kiss on the neck, picked up my eldest daughter and laughed: Ramón's yellow glasses, can you believe

it? His blue ones? His yellow house? And we put the girls to sleep, my wife went to bed, and me, I stayed in the living room, watching television, flipping channels, thinking.

'What will you do with it all?' my wife asked before she left. She leaned in the doorway, already in her nightclothes, and I could see the graceful outline of her body beneath the fabric. She was barefoot, her toes curling into the thick carpet.

'I was thinking we should move there,' I said, just to hear her horrified laughter.

She disappeared into the bedroom without saying goodnight.

'Did you know them well?' I asked Carlotta.

She thought about this for a second. 'They were my neighbours.'

'But did you know them?'

'I saw them every day,' she said.

And this means a good deal, I know it does. There was a time when I saw him every week, and we were closer then, maybe even something like brothers. 'Ramón and I grew up together. And then we lost touch.'

'You look tired,' Carlotta said. 'Why don't you sit? It might make you feel better.'

But I didn't want to, not yet. I went to the record player, lifting the dull plastic dustcover. A few dozen old LPs leaned against the wall and I thumbed through them: they were my grandfather's opera records. I put one on, a woman's elegant voice warbled through the room and, just like that, this melody I hadn't heard in so long – decades – dropped my temperature and made the ceiling seem very far above me, at an unnatural height. Carlotta tapped her toe to the music, though it seemed utterly rhythmless to me. It was true: I didn't feel well.

'What did people think of them in the neighbourhood?' I asked.

'Everyone loved them.'

'But no one knew them?'

'We didn't have to know them.'

And I thought about that, as the singing went on in Italian, a

lustrous female voice, and I was struck by the image of the two of them – Ramón and Matilde – sitting on this very same couch, my aunt whispering translations directly in his ear. Love songs, songs about desperate passion, about lovers who died together. I could almost see it: his smile lighting up this drab room, Matilde's lips pressed against him. They had died that way, best friends, strolling hand in hand off the edge of a bridge, until they sank. I sat down on the throw rug, leaning back against the sofa, staring ahead at an unadorned wall. My feet were very cold. My eyes had adjusted to the light now and the house seemed almost antiseptic. Clean. Preposterously dustless for this part of the city. We sat listening to the aria, Carlotta and I, a melody spiralling out into the infinite. The singer had such energy, and the more she drew upon it, the weaker I felt. I could stay here, I might never leave. I could inherit this life my uncle had left behind, walk away, I thought, from my old man and his venom.

'My father did everything he could to ruin my uncle,' I said. 'He cheated him out of his inheritance. He's in prison now, where he belongs.'

'I know. I read about him today in the paper. They talked to him.'

For a moment I thought I had misheard. 'What? Which paper?'

I turned to see Carlotta smiling proudly. Perhaps she hadn't heard the terror in my voice. Already I'd begun imagining all the horrible things my father might say, the conspiracy theories, the racist remarks, the angry insults with which he might have desecrated the memory of his dead brother.

'I don't remember the name of it,' Carlotta said. 'The same one I was in.'

'What did my father say?'

'There were journalists all over the neighbourhood yesterday. My son was on television. Did you see him?'

I raised my voice, suddenly impatient: 'But what did he say?'

'Mr Cano,' Carlotta whispered.

Her shoulders were hunched and she had leaned back into the

couch, as if to protect herself, as if I might attack her. I realized, with horror, that I had frightened her. She knew who my father was. I stammered an apology.

She took a deep breath now. 'He said he didn't have a brother. That he didn't know anyone named Ramón.'

'That's all?' I asked, and Carlotta nodded.

'No one named Ramón,' I said to myself, 'no brother.'

She stared at me like I was crazy. How could I explain that it didn't sound like him, that it was too sober, too calm?

'Why would he say that?' Carlotta asked.

I shook my head. I felt my eyes getting heavier. Was it cruel or just right?

'We should go,' I said. 'I'm very sorry, there's nothing here I need.' But it wasn't true and I couldn't leave. We sat, not speaking, not moving, only breathing, until I became aware that Carlotta was patting my head with a maternal affection, that my shoulders were sinking further toward the floor, and I gave in to it: loosened my tie, wiggling my toes in my socks, my feet frozen, the chill having spread through my body now. This record will not end, I thought, I hoped, but then it did: a long, fierce note held without the orchestra, culminating in a shout of joy from the singer, the audience chastened, stunned by the beauty of it. A long silence and then, slowly, applause, soft at first, then waves of it, which on this old recording came across like a pounding rain. I was shivering. There was no question we were underwater. ∎

SAVING THE WORLD

Tahmima Anam

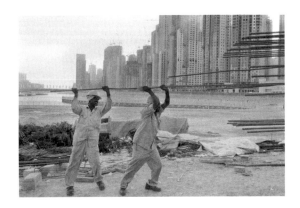

Bacchu

Today, my brothers, Mohammed and Rubel, are going to foreign. Mohammed is going to Africa and he wears a very handsome uniform.

(Our mother has died.)

Rubel wears an orange jumpsuit.

On the river island where we live, the water has turned to salt. The fish have disappeared, and only the shrimps are left. Mohammed has a lucky forehead, so he is going to foreign, and Rubel, whose forehead is unlucky, is also going to foreign, because he wants to be like Mohammed, and not take money from Mohammed, and marry his girl Komola.

Rubel went to work on the shrimp farm, but the money was no good, and he wants to get married, so he said, *I will go to Dubai, where so many young men have gone.* Then Mohammed said, *I am the oldest, I will send you the marriage money*, but Rubel said no because he will not take our brother's money.

(Our forty days of mourning have just ended.)

It is time to say goodbye. Our father says, *Go, Allah goes with you.*

Rubel

Go and earn in foreign, Komola's father said. *Then I will consider your proposal.* Then he added, *But not too long, eh? She'll have to be married soon.*

Damned either way.

We're at the airport, Mohammed and me. In his soldier uniform, the cap, the boots, he looks like a fucking prince. He shows me his pass. UNITED NATIONS PEACEKEEPING. My blood is hot with jealousy but I act like it's nothing, just another river boy going abroad to send home the cash, like the rest of us. Doesn't matter if you wear an army uniform or a jumpsuit, it's all the same. Cash, work, cash.

Only I remember the look on our mother's face when she first saw Mohammed in his uniform. And no way Komola's father would have rejected me if I was wearing it. He would have shown some respect. And I would have had a gun.

Mohammed

I am lucky to be here. Boys from river islands do not enlist in the Bangladesh Army. They are not taught to fire arms and travel to Africa. At my mother's insistence, I had one year of schooling. At school I demonstrated an aptitude. She persuaded my father to give me another year, and then another. I took the army entrance exam, and passed. I have been far from home ever since, living in army quarters, completing my training in Dhaka. My mother, may she rest in peace, could not hide the fact that I was her favourite. My returns to the island

have been awkward. Each time, she insisted on forcing Bacchu and Rubel to leave their beds so I could have the mosquito net to myself.

I must admit I knew very little about Africa before we set off, and when we arrive, I am surprised to find that the landscape of this country is not so different from my own. The trees have very thick leaves, and the air is humid. On the walls of our mess, the same green lizards skip across the tube lights.

Many people have already died in the long civil war – millions, we are told. And now there is a tentative peace, though there are some regions in the east where the fighting continues. It is to this eastern province that we are sent. We are peacekeepers, we are not here to fight. Still we carry arms and travel in convoys.

In a place called Bunia we set up camp. A few miles away there is a refugee settlement, where we will be tending to those who have fled the fighting.

I receive my first letter from home. Bacchu writes to say that the rain has caused a leak in our tin roof, which he has mended. He wants me to know that he is taking care of our father in my absence. There is news from Rubel, who has been assigned to a building project on an island called The World.

I wish Rubel were in the army with me. I persuaded him to take the entrance exam. When I was on leave, I taught him the lessons. He was adept – the sums came especially quickly to him. But he was not successful. Perhaps he became nervous. I was not present when it happened, but on my next leave Rubel was altered. He woke before dawn and left for the shrimp farm, staying away until after our hurricane lamps were lit. I heard he met a girl. I offered to send extra money, but he refused. And then the owner of the shrimp farm, Khan Shaheb, took a liking to the same girl. We all believed it would be best to give up the connection, but Rubel insisted he would marry that girl and no other.

Rubel

If I wasn't looking at it with my own eyes I wouldn't believe it. I'm not a praying man but I wonder what God would say if he knew people were pulling out the sea and making land. *Dubai is a small country,* the guy next to me says, *with big money.* With money, you can turn the sea into the land and make a small country into a big country. The guy's name is Asif. *Where you from?* he asks me. *Sirajganj,* I say, and he says, *I'm from Dhaka,* like it's the centre of the fucking planet.

All day Asif and me and about a hundred other guys are carrying sand on our heads from one place to another. This is what we have been brought here to do: make fake islands out of sand. The giant dredgers pull the earth from under us, dragging fish and rocks and bits of the ocean floor, and when that is done we will be building a hotel. Grand Island Hotel – Your Home in The World.

I'm here two months and no word, nothing from Komola.

Bacchu

NGO lady says the water is heating up so this year the flood will come early, and stay longer and rise higher and sink us all, which does not seem to bother my father. He has bought a new Xian Chinese television with the money that my brothers have sent. *Where will you see your programmes?* I ask him. Our cousin in the next village has no electric. But he is too busy watching *Notun Kuri.*

(I wish I was Chinese. I cannot stop dreaming about what my life would be like if I was Chinese. I heard there was a flood in China, and you know what they did? New houses for everyone, on higher ground, so that next year they were not in the way. No more drowning Chinks.)

If it floods the television will be carried away along with the house, the bed, our clothes and our goat. When I pointed this out to Father he said God would not strike the same place twice. I thought (but

did not say), this is not a real place, it is a riverbank, and if the river were to overflow on to the Xian it would only be fulfilling its duty as a river.

Mohammed

I have received a telegram from home. The rains have come early, and the waters are rising in the village. Bacchu writes to ask me what they should do. *Please advise*, the telegram says. I wonder how he has reached the post office to send the telegram. The boy is intelligent, but he is young.

The camp here is filling with more people escaping the fighting. Every day we meet hollow-eyed women and children. I have known poverty at home, but nothing has prepared me for the sight of these refugees, so many of them. I am repulsed by the flies clinging to their eyelids. The smell of death is overpowering.

Not for the first time, I want to go home.

Rubel

I want to go home. Still no letters from Komola. The night before I left, she let me kiss her. Her lips were bitter. When I scowled at the taste, she laughed and told me she'd been in the fields, making oil from the mustard flowers.

All this way I have travelled for a girl. *Earn in foreign*, I keep hearing her father's voice; *earn in foreign earn in foreign.*

I am convinced her father has made her marry Khan. The thought stirs up a rage in me, and I move faster through the line, carrying the sand on my head, and Asif tells me to slow down, *You're running ahead of everyone*, but I am thinking of Khan.

I do this sometimes when I am very tired: think of Khan lifting Komola's veil, planting a kiss on her cheek – just to wake up in the morning in my fish-stink bunk, pull on my uniform, ignore its curdled smell...

Khan and Komola, mounting the wedding dais; he looks at her in

the mirror with hungry eyes

Lift, twist, mix, lever

He cups her breast in his palm; a soft, unmolested palm; she likes it. He smells of leisure

Hammer, sledge, pivot, rivet, sparks, pump, muscle, muscle, muscle

I'm going to save the money for a ticket and go home. I'll hire myself out as a day labourer, work in the fields, move to Dhaka, slave at the clothes machine – anything.

Bacchu

The water is rising but my father does not take his eyes from the television. Since the funeral, he never takes his eyes from the television. He is ignoring everything, so every day I have to take the money to the market and buy the rice and cook and wash the plates. NGO lady tells me we have to leave the village but Father is settled in his bed as though nothing can touch him while the television is on. At three o'clock we watch *Notun Kuri*. At four o'clock *Khobor*. We are watching *Khobor* when the water comes to the door. By the time the programme is over the water is lapping at the doorway and the two mud steps to our house have already washed away.

I shut off the generator and pack the Xian into a tin trunk. My father is shouting and I am stuffing leaves into the trunk and promising it will stay dry, and he is throwing his fist into the sky as though he can make it stop raining, but nothing can stop the river when it is about to break its banks, not even God.

Rubel

Calling the island The World gives our bosses the impression they are doing something important, something better than pushing our sweaty backs from one end of the desert to another. It makes them ignore the stink and the sun crashing into our bodies.

The worst thing is, the bastards are holding our wages. For the first

six months, we didn't see a paisa. When we worked up the guts to grumble, they sent a man who showed us a piece of paper with lines and numbers. The writing wasn't in Bangla. It wasn't even in English. *None of you read Arabic?* he said, acting like we were all a bunch of no-good Muslims who hadn't even bothered to learn the Holy Tongue.

Saleem, one of our guys who started wearing white and referring to Allah like he was his best friend the moment we stepped foot in Dubai, said in his meekest voice, *Sir, I am learning to read the Holy Book.*

Mahshallah, the man said. And then he said, *This chart here shows your earnings. These are your expenses, what the company invested on your behalf.*

But we paid for our passage, I said, *tickets, uniforms, everything.*

If you could read it, he said, *you would see that the company has spent good money on your employment. You think all of this* – he points to the wormhole where we sleep – *comes cheap? Your salary will be paid to you in due course.*

As soon as I get my money I am getting out and I am marrying Komola.

Mohammed

I am holding my rifle as steadily as I can as our jeep bumps over the road. It is not much more than a dirt track, with fields of high grass on either side. The raw sun beats upon us. It is hot and silent but I am shivering. My palms are slick and the rifle begins to slip.

I see my mother in a field. *Stop*, I say, *stop now*. We are at the end of the convoy. *Stop now*, I repeat. Everyone turns around and sees my mother. They tell me to go out and get her. The rest of the convoy continues on.

I step out of the jeep and walk towards her. Behind me, the men train

their rifles over my head. The woman's face comes into focus and I can see that she is waving a length of green cloth. She is not my mother, only a woman in a long African dress. Now as I am running towards her my foot nudges something soft on the ground.

I hold my gun in the air, and just as I reach the woman I hear the sound of firing ahead. Our jeep lurches forward and the other men tumble out. There is shouting, and the smell of fire. I hold the woman, not my mother, and we fall into the grasses, and there, woven into the dirt, are children, dozens and dozens of children, lying with their eyes open and their mouths open.

Bacchu

Rubel has sent me a letter. From the stamp I can see that it has taken two months to reach me, which is not a long time if you think about how long it took for NGO lady to reach us after our house was washed away. (Three days we sat on the roof, and all the time my father was crying about the Xian, and asking, again and again, if I was sure the trunk was sound.)

I tear the letter open because I am hoping it is the photograph of the Great Wall of China that I have asked Rubel to send but instead there is a photograph of himself in the orange jumpsuit standing on the beach. He is smiling and grabbing his waist like a film star.

I have a very important job for you. Now you are old enough, I am entrusting you with this task and you must not fail me.

Rubel

We got our money today. Now I have to get my passport from the supervisor.

He is right up in my face when he tells me there is absolutely no way I can leave now. His breath is disgusting, like old shoes. I try to act sweet, even though the stink is making me want to spit into his fat yellow eyes, and I say, *Please, sir, I need to get married.* He laughs. Then he says, *Under no circumstances can you retire before your*

contract is complete.

I know a guy, Asif says, *takes care of situations like yours.* He is grinning and I know he's about to get me into something serious. I imagine myself being thrown in jail, and for a moment I am about to say no, but then I think of Komola, and before I know it we are at the photo studio and Asif is saying, *Try to look smart, like you're not the kind of guy who would try to go home with a fake passport.*

Mohammed

Our men are strewn about the road, some of them torn to pieces. We find a few alive, staunch their wounds with our hands. The smell of burning flesh is biting. I try to explain about the children, but no one is listening. The woman in the field has saved my life. If she had not appeared when she did, our jeep would have been caught in the ambush.

We return to Bunia with the dead and the injured. We find a translator and the woman is questioned. *They came at dawn,* she says in Swahili. *They shot the children and took the men, then they came back and waited. They waited for you to drive past.* She mentions her father's village. It is half an hour's journey. Her name is Sakina. And then she says, *Take me away from here.*

Bacchu

My brother Rubel writes that under no circumstances can I allow Komola to marry Khan. *Under no circumstances.* Otherwise no job in Dubai for me. (If I can't get to Dubai I can't get to China and if I can't get to China I can't become a Chinese and if I can't become a Chinese I will drown in this country like everyone else.)

Komola's father looks at me kindly. *Good boy,* he says, *have you come to give your blessing? Come here, sit beside me.*

His house is as drowned as our house and the only place to sit is on the fallen trunk of a tree. I squat on the mud, dragging the trunk behind me.

What's this? he says. *Did your father send you?*
I am fiddling with the lock. *Under no circumstances.* The trunk lock is rusty. (I had to tell Father that the trunk was lost, that it floated away with the rest of our things.)

Finally I give the lock a hard pull and it gives way, but I don't lift the lid because I have rehearsed it exactly and I have to say the line first before I can show Komola's father the television.

My brother Rubel has sent a marriage proposal to your daughter, Komola. Please accept this gift

(flourish)

as a sign of his serious nature and his

The blow strikes me solid on the head. *GET OUT GET OUT GET OUT,* he shouts. His face is purple and his hand is purple as he points to the trunk. The Xian is sitting in a puddle, and worse, the leaves have covered it with a thick slimy coating. You can't even tell what it is, it just looks like a box full of mud.

I try to explain. *TEEVEE TEEVEE TEEVEE,* I shout, waving the photograph of Rubel, but he is slapping me away, cursing twelve generations of my family.

Mohammed

The dead soldiers are placed in coffins. My salute is unsteady as they are loaded on to an aeroplane, our anthem playing in the background. I think of their wives, and their mothers, and I think of Sakina, who has lost her children.

She comes to the barracks. I cannot understand her words, except the first two. *Thank you.* I shake my head to mean, you're welcome. I speak to her in Bengali, she speaks to me in her tongue. Understanding nothing of what she says, I begin to tell her the story of Razia Sultana, the Mughal Queen who loved an African. I cannot say exactly why I am telling her this story.

Perhaps only to remind myself that our people have known one another a long time.

Bacchu

We are attending the wedding of Khan Shaheb and Komola. Father had to beg their forgiveness for my behaviour. *Little one didn't know what he was doing*, Father pleaded, *mother dead less than a year. Mother dead, brothers are in foreign, poor boy lost his head.* So they have forgiven me and we are eating biryani at the wedding like everyone else. Komola is crying into her hands, but everyone is thinking that is what an obedient bride should do: cry on the dais, cry as she touches her father's feet, cry as they take her away. But they are also thinking: thanks to her, the shrimp farmer is feeding the entire village. The meat is so delicious I almost forget about my brother.

(I eat as slowly as I can, and dream of China.)

Rubel

At the airport I wear a suit, but by the time I reach the immigration desk my armpits are swimming and my forehead is soaked. The man behind the desk peers at me. *Where are you going?* he says. *Home,* I reply. *I'm getting married.*

He waits a long time, the bastard, before saying, *Congratulations.*

Stamp, Stamp.

Mohammed

Sakina comes back the next day. I have just returned from another patrol, and I am washing the grit out of my hair. She stands and stares as I run my head under the tap. Then she reaches for me and takes the soap from my hand. Her fingers are in my hair, pulling out the small bits of sand, and the foam swims into my eyes.

We sleep in a motel. Her breasts taste of milk. I lay my head against her stomach and, for the first time since coming to Africa, I weep for my mother. ∎

IN MEMORY OF SIMON GRAY

The former editor of *Granta*, and the editor of Simon Gray's
'Smoking Diaries' trilogy, remembers him.

Ian Jack

S imon Gray was born on October 21, 1936, and died on the
evening of August 6, 2008. He'd been expecting to die; his family
and friends knew he was dying; it was the quickness that took us by
surprise – he died, suddenly, from an aneurysm. In our last
conversation, a few weeks before, he said he was suffering from
'pseudo gout' – 'Agony. God knows what genuine gout must be like'
– but of course gout was just one in a series of secondary maladies
that were easier to talk about than the lung cancer that was killing
him. Simon's lung cancer was predictable, but the truth of that
statement is somehow offensive to his memory and his
accomplishments, as though the most important thing about Freud
was that he smoked too many cigars and had cancer in the jaw.
Simon started smoking when he was a boy of eight or nine and
continued to smoke for more than sixty years, latterly Silk Cut and
at his smoking peak at least three packs a day. His ultimate diagnosis
and prognosis merely allowed him to carry on with a surer fatalism
– no point in stopping now, so far down the motorway past the slip
road. It wasn't that he 'loved' smoking, as some people say they do,
or even that he enjoyed it very much. It was just that he needed to –
a genetic and cultural disposition to nicotine that came from the time
when a pipe-and-fag fug lay over every English living room, an age
that his parents perfectly characterized. When we talked in July I
asked him about the current number. Ten a day maybe? A reluctant
sigh. 'Oh no, double that, probably.' We promised to meet for supper
in September, when we'd both be back in London from holiday.

Meals with Simon were always a treat, but they needed careful
arranging. He rose too late for lunch to be a possibility, but supper
brought its problems, too, because as an ex-drinker – a doctor told
him if he didn't stop he'd be dead within days – he liked to eat early
and drink Diet Coke in exactly the right way, cold and bubbling from

the bottle, when its texture is closest to champagne's. Abstinence from alcohol also left him with a sugar craving, so the restaurant's sweets needed to be good. If conditions were perfect, or if the imperfect ones could be ignored, Simon would give a good impersonation of a man having an excellent time on Diet Coke and chocolate ice cream at 6.45 in the evening. He was a generous conversationalist and a generous emailer, by which I mean he was spontaneous and unguarded and not a cultivated ironist. Once in a restaurant he looked across the room towards a reasonably famous novelist. 'That crowd are all so watchful and with-held,' he said. 'I wonder what they've got to be so with-held about?' Simon's writing was informed by professional disappointment, age, literature, lost friends and brothers, and illness. The wise comedy and almost incontinent honesty of his last four books came out of these things, forever squawking around and finding rest in his one constant balm, his wife. In my view they will still find readers a hundred years from now, but I write as his former editor.

I first met him in the 1970s, when in every sense he was in his champagne years as one of the most successful playwrights writing for the English stage. All that changed, in ways his books describe far better than anyone else can. When I met him again at a publishing party seven or eight years ago he said he had written something; would I like to see it? 'I should warn you it isn't properly written – full stops, verbs and so forth. It's full of dashes and stuff.' A typescript arrived after several months. Many dashes and oddly placed semi-colons – but a thrilling sense of a writer making a memoir do something brilliant and original. It was very funny. We ran the piece in the magazine and soon after Simon delivered the entire book, which he'd called 'I, Solipsist'. It became *The Smoking Diaries,* to be followed by *The Year of the Jouncer, The Last Cigarette,* and soon to be published, posthumously, *Coda,* from which the extract that follows is taken.

There may be better accounts of that frightening prospect that lies in wait for so many of us – knowing (while trying not to know) how little time one has to live – but I have never read one. This, you feel, is what it must be like. ∎

CODA

Simon Gray

Pleasantries and Other Pleasures

It's a heavenly day. Warm, with the mildest of breezes, the sea calm and the surrounding mountains visible, with the distinct hint, like large thoughts not yet thought, of mountains beyond them, and beyond. I'm sitting at the table, as has become my habit, with my back resting against the chapel wall. In front of me are the tables and chairs of the restaurant, and then the esplanade and the steps down to the beach. It's the sort of day that helps people to be friends, almost everyone who passes by me nods or smiles, some say a few words, the routine words – 'Isn't it lovely here!' and 'What a beautiful day,' or more personally, 'You look comfortable there in the shade.' An elderly Scotsman with a verra thick accent has just loitered to discuss the charms of the hotel, it's his first time in Greece, usually he goes to Portugal 'and such', he tries to learn the language of the country he holidays in, but he's finding Greek 'verra, verra difficult' – he's been here a week, going back on Tuesday, so he doubts that

he'll master it on this visit, at least – Well, it was a nice conversation, cheerful and easy. Then he was down to the beach and a few minutes later up again with a stately, heavy-treading silver-haired wife, who continued on her way while he paused to tell me to send him a cheque, a blank cheque, any sort of cheque would do as long as it was blank. I laughed and nodded, but couldn't think what to say because I didn't understand the joke, if it was a joke. Yes, it was a joke, his countenance and the tone of his voice announced it as such, but what was its point? I'm going to go for a swim, why not?

Victoria was on the beach, lolling on a sunbed, reading. I sidled up to her, reached for her hand to lead her into the sea, but coughed before I could surprise her. That's the thing about this cough. It's not the free and easy, loose and phlegmy, and on the whole controllable cough of health. It's a tight little cough, a bit of a rasper, that comes when it chooses. It's a cancer cough, as the swelling on my neck is a cancer swelling, one the audible, the other the visible sign of my condition.

Victoria has become used to the cough. As soon as she heard it she looked up, then held out her hand – and so, though I didn't succeed in surprising her, I did nevertheless lead her into the sea, which was clear and still, with only one other couple swimming, but lots of small black fish scampering near the surface. We sported about in the shallows, as I haven't yet the courage to go out of my depth. I'm not sure of my strength, whether it won't suddenly give out, as it's started to do now and then on land, when I have to pause, stoop to recover my breath, my legs heavy and weak, my shoulders sagging. If that happens in the water I can probably roll on to my back and float. On the other hand, well, there are worse deaths, some of them in bed.

Eventually Victoria went off for a proper swim and I stayed near the shore, the water just up to my neck. If I bent my knees I had the feeling of being suspended. It was really very pleasant, hanging about in the water, watching her steady breaststroke taking her away from

me until the fuzz of her hair was too far out for my liking. The familiar anxiety clutched at my heart, and, as if responding to it, she turned and headed back. We got out – a nice, easy beach to get out on to, thank God – and went to the shower, an unusual shower in that it delivers the water with such force that it hits the skin like needles, and the top of one's head is sore for a few moments afterwards. Then she returned to the sunbed and her book, and I walked to the steps, intending to come back here to the chapel. But I didn't come back here, I turned around, and without actually concealing myself from Victoria slipped back into the water without her seeing me. I think I wanted to test myself out. I did all the things I've been doing since I was five or six, underwater somersaults, spiral dives, corkscrews. I went through my repertoire grimly, as if I were auditioning, then more and more freely until suddenly, without at first being conscious of it, I was enjoying myself – splashing and sporting, diving and twirling, holding my breath underwater for quite long stretches. Then I did the more taxing stuff, the two backstrokes, the sidestroke and the crawl. The backstrokes were fine, the sidestroke OK, but the crawl wasn't right. Something was out of alignment, in the small of my back or at the base of my spine. And the fact is that although I could do all the other strokes properly, I couldn't do any of them for very long, almost as if, when it came to purposeful swimming, my body had a weak will or a short attention span – it's not that I slowed down or wore myself out, I just stopped – perhaps it was to catch my breath, perhaps my lungs had abruptly emptied. But that's all right, really, perfectly all right, because I had so much pleasure from the breath that kept me afloat – yes, think of it that way, a new way, for you, of thinking about things.

As I was writing the above a young Frenchman with a perpetual half-smile and a perpetual stubble – it's been the same length for three days now, how does he do it? – stopped by to confide that he was leaving this afternoon, he was very sad, going back home to Tours, did I know Tours? I said I did, which was a lie, and a foolish

one – my plan was to stop him telling me about Tours, its history, its architecture, its restaurants, after all there would be no need for him to tell me if he thought that I already knew – but he was so astonished that I knew Tours that he wanted to know when I'd been, why, and what did I think of it? So I said, 'Oh,' I said, 'it was a long time ago, and it might have been Lourdes, come to think of it, yes, Lourdes, not Tours.' He did a polite little French gape, eyebrows up, mouth pursed, at the thought that anyone, even an Englishman, could confuse going to Lourdes with going to Tours, but then pressed on to what he really wanted to talk about, which was his new car. He was picking it up in Paris on his way to Tours, it was an English car, a beautiful car, it was a Jaguar!

'Wow!' I said.

We beamed proudly at each other, he because of his new car, I because I come from the country that made it. Then he passed on, up the path to the hotel and – I think I can say with confidence, though of course you never know – out of my life for ever. He's not somebody I would mind meeting again, he was so friendly and pleased with everything.

Doctor Number Three: Chipmunk of Doom

I was just about to settle back against the wall of the chapel, stop writing for a while and smoke what would be only my third cigarette of the day. Only! Only your third! Yes well but – three months ago it would have been my twenty-third, thirtieth even – no, it wouldn't, it's not midday yet, three months ago you wouldn't even have been up, so you wouldn't have smoked any cigarettes, none – I've actually managed to put the cigarette back in the pack, but in order to keep it there I've got to go on writing, and I don't really want to, as I'll almost certainly find myself writing about the third doctor, the one that came after Omar and Morgan Morgan, the one I keep putting off writing about –

He wore the same sort of clothes as Omar and Morgan Morgan, dark suit, shirt, tie, but in their cases the clothes seemed both to confer authority and to imply deference. I think I described Omar as looking like an undertaker, and though Morgan Morgan gave the impression of being dishevelled the dishevelment was in his personality, he was still in absolutely the right clothes, the clothes were right for the man and the clothes were right for the job, ergo the man was right for the job, was how it worked in the cases of both Omar and Morgan Morgan. The third doctor looked wrong in all three respects, though my first impression, physical and before thought, was that he was a chipmunk, a massive chipmunk, and then the second one, when he'd formed into a man, that he was in the wrong clothes, that they were too grown-up for him. In fact, he looked like an exuberant prep-school boy, circa the period I went to prep school. His eyes popped boisterously behind the lenses of large spectacles, his straw-coloured hair stood straight up from his head as if in jubilation, and his round, pink face wore a worried, an actively worried, expression, as if knowing that it wasn't the expression required, which should have been responsible, grave, kindly, an expression along those lines. All through the conversation he gave the impression of being simultaneously surprised and at a loss, as if he'd been caught out doing something not exactly against the rules, but against some code he wasn't yet quite grown-up enough to understand. So when he said, once he'd got behind his desk, that he was very sorry, it really did sound as if he was apologising for some misdemeanour of his own, which prevented it from being the chillingly serious opening that he'd probably intended it to be. He probably wanted to start from an absolutely clear understanding of my situation – that it demanded and deserved profound commiserations, and we would proceed from there.

In fact, we didn't seem to be proceeding towards much of consequence. He pretty well repeated what Omar and Morgan Morgan had said – i.e. there were two possibilities: 1) that the tumour on my neck was an independent tumour, the two tumours

could be treated separately, in both cases either by surgery or by chemotherapy; 2) that the tumour on the neck was a secondary of the tumour in my lung, which would mean that the cancer cells were in my bloodstream, and the treatment, by radiotherapy, would be palliative, a matter of keeping the cancer in check, but not curing it. The question as to whether we were confronted by 1) or 2) would be answered by the operation to be performed by Dr Morgan Morgan – 'Now, is there anything you want to ask me?' It came out very abruptly, not at all the hesitant invitation of Omar and Morgan Morgan. It was almost a challenge. There was a brief pause, during which he – let me give him a name – Len Rootle let me call him, Dr Rootle – So –

'Now, is there anything you want to ask me?' asked Dr Rootle.

Then came the brief pause. During it he sat behind his desk ogling us. We indicated that there was nothing we wanted to ask him.

'Well,' he said, 'would you like a prognosis? I mean, if the operation to be performed by Dr Morgan Morgan doesn't reveal a cancer in the throat, would you like a prognosis?' It was most peculiar, most peculiar, the way he got this out, awkward, impetuous and alarmed, with a throb of excitement in it.

'No,' Victoria said firmly. No, for her part, she certainly, most certainly didn't want to hear a prognosis.

Dr Rootle nodded inattentively, his ogle was fixed on me.

The word 'prognosis' made me dizzy. Especially as we hadn't yet had a definitive diagnosis, which couldn't be made until after Dr Morgan Morgan's operation, surely – how long would it take them after Dr Morgan Morgan's operation to reach a definitive diagnosis? I wondered.

'How long –' I began, and stopped, thinking that I didn't really want to prolong the conversation, really it was time to go home. Dr Rootle decided that 'How long?' was the whole of my question, which was in response to his own question, so, yes please, he took me to mean, give me your prognosis, how long do I have before I die? 'About a year.' The words came out of the side of his mouth, low but clear.

I believe I said, 'Christ!' I looked at Victoria, who shrank, looked small and white.

I wanted to say, 'But I didn't ask that question, so kindly withdraw your answer.' I also wanted to swear at him, 'You stupid fucking awful fucking moron' sort of stuff, and for a moment or two, as I stared at his face, now for the first time befittingly calm and solemn, with a certain satisfaction in it – 'Mission accomplished! Difficult deed done, and out of the side of my mouth too!' – I wanted to kill him. I wanted to kill him and say just as I pulled the trigger, thrust the dagger, whatever, 'That's a year longer than you have, matey.' The thing I think I understood immediately, before I'd even thought about it, was that a doctor who tells you that you have a year to live has taken the year away from you – from the moment the sentence was delivered – the sentence that delivered the sentence – the knowledge would never be cleared from my consciousness, the last thought at night, the first in the morning, for the rest of my life –

I really don't remember much about how it went after that.

My Struggle to Escape – Part One

It is one o'clock in the morning, I am sitting at a table on the patio that separates our room from our small private swimming pool, and I am becoming maddened by the walls that hem me in. At the end of the pool there is a row of jagged rocks, cemented together with a gap in the middle to give a view of the sea, which is pitch black. In the morning it's the most marvellous blue, the sea stretches out, you can see boats in the distance, and there is a sense of space, ease, freedom and I leap into the pool, naked, and swim about – this morning, for instance, we went to the beach and swam in the sea, it was almost transparent, it was lovely, then walked back along the garden paths to our room, to find breakfast on the table I am now writing at. I took off my trunks and into the pool I went. It's a saltwater pool, quite cold, cold and cramped, and I don't quite know why I do it, especially after a proper swim in the sea, but it's now become a ritual – sea swim, pool

swim, shower, breakfast, and over breakfast the view of the sparkling blue, and the yachts and their sails –

But at night I feel trapped by the walls, the blackness of the sea, so impenetrably black, no lights of passing ships, nothing to distinguish it from the black sky, and my lungs feel as if they are contracting, I begin to cough and wheeze, and panic sets in – panic is setting in now, as I write – I find myself hating the hotel that I like so much in the daytime, and particularly hating the manager –

The wall to the right is so high that it is impossible to see over it. The wall to the left is lower, and if I stand up I can see into the neighbouring pool and the patio and even into a bit of the room next door, and beyond, over their low wall, I can see all the way to the beach, and the little chapel where I sit writing in the daytime, and then the hill above the hotel, with the lights of the cars moving along the roads – the sea is bright, little boats bobbing up and down, and the waves rippling – it is a charming and a painful sight – painful because now I passionately covet the room next to ours that commands this view from its patio, and this morning we were offered it by the manager, and I turned it down. Why did I? Why did he let me? Why didn't he insist on my taking it? What a fool I am! Fool! Sitting here at the table, in my pitch-black cell, my cancer cell – this is hysteria.

That was hysteria.

I calmed down by going to the wall I could see over, the left wall, and breathing in the view, the beach, the little white chapel where I sit, the hills and the lights moving up and down and across. Then I came back here, to the table, and smoked a cigarette.

Now I'm going to write it down in a sensible fashion.

The reason I didn't accept the next-door room that I now covet only just this side of lunacy is because the manager wouldn't let us have a rather splendid bungalow on the other side of the hotel, with accommodation for six people, with the swimming pool set on a large

lawn, and most importantly, from the patio where I would sit at night, there was an expansive view of the sea. It's been unoccupied for several days, according to the young Italian couple in the small suite next to it, and will probably remain unoccupied until the end of the season, and is very expensive, expensive even for four, therefore preposterously expensive for two. I asked the manager if he would give us a discount – no, let's get this absolutely right, for some reason I was worried that he would be upset – his feelings would be hurt – if we wanted to change rooms without explanation, he would think we didn't like our room, which, he'd confided to me, was the best room in the hotel, the one that he, personally, liked the most – he's a rather freaky looking guy, about fifty I suppose, short, with a rosy complexion and glistening black eyes and black plastered-back hair and a high-pitched voice – a lot of Cretans, we've noticed, have high-pitched voices and are quite short – he wears trousers that look as if they're made of tweed, hitched high up on his body, to almost his armpits, and has a rapid, disjointed walk. When we arrived at the hotel last Sunday, at around midnight, it was pouring with rain. A savage wind lashed at us as we got out of the taxi. He came dashing out of the rather grand entrance into the rain and wind to welcome us with an umbrella and to escort us down to an empty restaurant, where a meal had been arranged. The hotel has four restaurants that all close before 11 p.m., which is depressing and completely un-Greek, in our experience, but still, it was thoughtful of him to have a meal ready and waiting, though actually it was spooky, the two of us sitting there in an otherwise totally empty restaurant, the wind howling, the rain beating at the large glass doors.

A very nice man in a suit, plump and avuncular, though about twenty years younger than me, a maître d' figure, I suppose, brought us an assortment of dishes I couldn't eat, so Victoria had to be politely hungry for two. 'Oh, my fran, no food, why no food?' the maître d' kept saying, gazing miserably down at my untouched plate and caressing my shoulder until I was desperate to get away from him, his wounded eyes and the threat of further dishes – perhaps he'd

cooked them himself – and said how tired we were, sleepy, and backed it up with imitations of myself sleeping, snoring noises and so forth, but still he insisted on bringing us some terrible Greek puddings. It was a great relief when the manager reappeared, and we could leave the table with fulsome thank yous to the maître d' and scurry after the manager through the rain to our room. It was then that he told me of his love for it, that it was his favourite room etc. and it was just after he'd gone, while Victoria was unpacking, that I took in these oppressive walls. 'We can't stay here,' I said, although it was obvious that we'd have to, at least for the night –

which I got through by taking two sleeping pills, and two co-proxamol, and half a dozen cigarettes. I sat outside on the patio, not completely protected from the rain by a sliver of roofing, and not at all from the wind, which came whistling and howling through or over the walls in a way that seemed quite personal, as if it were seeking me out, in fact. 'Hey! Go get the cancer guy smoking his cigarettes. He's in a daze or a doze from his sleepers. See if you can shake him up a bit. Make him scream out or cry like when we did the old guy back on the heath. See if he's got any "Blow, winds, and crack your cheeks" sort of stuff in him. Cancer, cigarettes, chemicals. Talk about a deserving case!'

At some point before dawn I climbed into bed and clung to my wife. ∎

CONTRIBUTORS

Daniel Alarcón is associate editor of *Etiqueta Negra* and the author of two works of fiction, including *Lost City Radio*, named a best book of 2007 by the *Washington Post* and the *LA Times*. In 2007, he was chosen as one of *Granta*'s Best of Young American Novelists and his story, 'The King is Always Above the People', was published in *Granta* 97.

Tahmima Anam was born in Dhaka, Bangladesh, in 1975. Her debut novel, *A Golden Age*, received the 2008 Commonwealth Best First Book prize. Her short story, 'The Courthouse', appeared in *Granta* 96.

Carol Ann Duffy was born in Glasgow. She grew up in Stafford and then attended the University of Liverpool, where she studied philosophy. She has written for both children and adults, and her poetry has received many awards, including the Signal, the Whitbread and Forward prizes, as well as the E. M. Forster award in America.

Simon Gray was awarded a CBE in the 2005 New Year Honours list. He is the author of over thirty plays, including *Butley*, *The Common Pursuit* and *Cell Mates*. He has published several volumes of diaries and memoir, including *The Smoking Diaries*, *Enter a Fox*, *Fat Chance* and *The Last Cigarette*. 'Coda' is from a memoir of the same title, to be published by Faber and Granta Books in November 2008. A former contributing editor of this magazine, he died in August 2008.

Jennifer Haigh was born in Barnesboro, Pennsylvania in 1968. Her first novel, *Mrs. Kimble*, won the Hemingway Foundation/PEN Award for debut fiction and her second, *Baker Towers*, won the L.L. Winship/PEN New England Award. Her most recent novel is *The Condition*.

Aleksandar Hemon was born and raised in Sarajevo, Bosnia-Herzegovina and has lived in the USA since 1992. He is the author

of *The Question of Bruno, Nowhere Man* and *The Lazarus Project*. His short story 'Pronek in History' was published in *Granta* 72.

Elizabeth Lowry's first novel, *The Bellini Madonna*, has just been published.

Catherine O'Flynn is the author of *What Was Lost*, winner of the 2007 Costa First Novel Award.

Craig Raine's *Collected Poems 1978–1999* was published in 1999. He is the editor of *Areté* and he last appeared in *Granta* 100 with the poem 'How Snow Falls'. He has just finished a novel.

Lalage Snow spent a year documenting 1st Battalion Scots Guards and other regiments attached to them during their training, deployment and operations in Afghanistan and Iraq. She is working on a photographic book about the domestic environments of soldiers at war.

Binyavanga Wainaina is the founding editor of *Kwani?*, a Kenyan literary magazine. In 2009 he will be a Writing Fellow at Bard College. 'How to Write About Africa' was published in *Granta* 92. His first book, *Discovering Home*, will be published in 2008.

Richard Watson is an investigative journalist on BBC *Newsnight*. For the past eight years he has been *Newsnight*'s specialist reporter covering Islamist extremism and terrorism. His investigations have won him two Royal Television Society Awards.

Lois Williams grew up along the Wash in Norfolk and now lives in the United States. She is working on a book about the invention of home.

Contributing Editors
Diana Athill, Jonathan Derbyshire, Sophie Harrison, Isabel Hilton, Blake Morrison, Philip Oltermann, John Ryle, Sukhdev Sandhu, Lucretia Stewart.

GRANTA | 104

FATHERS
The Men Who Made Us

Four years after 'Mothers' *Granta* 104 set its sights on fathers: **Rawi Hage** conjures Beirut, as seen through his father's eyes; **Junot Díaz** takes on Latin America's 'Big Men'; and **Siri Hustvedt** meditates on family life. Plus: writers on photographs of their fathers, including **Isabel Fonseca**, **Ali Smith**, **Jon McGregor** and **Reina James**, who writes about life as the daughter of the comedian Sid James.

www.granta.com

Web exclusives: Dispatches from Cambodia and Lebanon; interviews with established and emerging writers; short films and audio discussions with *Granta* contributors; original fiction in our New Voices series; news, blogs, photography and highlights from the archive, updated daily.